CALEB ROSS

# Develop High Quality Video Games with c++ and Unreal

# Contents

# Introduction

*Overview of Game Development with C++ and Unreal Engine*

G ame development is an art form, a technical pursuit, and a storytelling medium all rolled into one. For decades, video games have evolved from simple 8-bit adventures to sprawling digital landscapes where every blade of grass sways under the weight of intricate physics simulations. Central to this evolution are the programming languages and development environments that empower creators to bring their visions to life. Among these, C++ and Unreal Engine stand tall as industry cornerstones.

**Why C++?**

C++ is a high-performance, general-purpose programming language known for its control over system resources, robust standard libraries, and object-oriented programming (OOP) features. It is a favorite among game developers for its speed, fine-tuned memory management, and versatility in creating complex, interactive environments. In game development, these characteristics are crucial for managing CPU and memory usage efficiently, which directly impacts the player experience.

When working with Unreal Engine, C++ isn't just an option; it's the backbone. Unreal Engine uses C++ to power its core functionalities, from physics calculations to rendering systems. While Unreal offers a visual scripting tool called *Blueprints*, many performance-critical elements and custom features require diving into C++. By mastering this language, you unlock the full power of the engine and its myriad capabilities.

**Why Unreal Engine?**

Unreal Engine is one of the most powerful and widely-used game development platforms in the world. Known for its high-end graphics capabilities, real-time rendering, and extensive toolsets, Unreal Engine empowers developers to create visually stunning games and interactive experiences. From blockbuster AAA titles to innovative indie projects, Unreal is the go-to choice for developers looking to push the boundaries of what games can achieve.

At its core, Unreal Engine provides developers with a comprehensive suite of tools and systems. Whether you're working on photorealistic environments, complex AI behaviors, or detailed character animations, Unreal offers specialized modules to cater to each requirement. With a flexible visual scripting language (Blueprints) and a robust C++ API, Unreal enables developers at all skill levels to build games ranging from simple prototypes to fully-featured commercial products.

## Key Features of Unreal Engine

- **Real-time Graphics and High Fidelity**: Unreal's rendering pipeline supports cutting-edge technologies like ray tracing, dynamic lighting, and physically-based materials, enabling photorealistic visuals.
- **Powerful Animation and Rigging Tools**: The engine comes equipped with advanced animation features such as blend spaces, root motion, and inverse kinematics (IK), crucial for creating fluid and realistic character movements.
- **Advanced Physics and Simulation**: Unreal's physics engine is ideal for realistic environmental interactions, collision handling, destructible environments, and cloth simulation.
- **Cross-Platform Deployment**: Unreal Engine supports a range of platforms including PC, consoles (PlayStation, Xbox, and Nintendo

Switch), mobile devices (iOS and Android), and emerging platforms such as VR/AR.

- **AI and Behavior Trees**: Unreal provides dedicated tools for creating intelligent NPCs using behavior trees, blackboards, and advanced pathfinding systems.

For any aspiring or seasoned developer, understanding the synergy between C++ and Unreal Engine is crucial. This combination allows developers to maximize performance, customize game features, and truly own their projects.

## The Purpose of This Book

The purpose of this book is to guide you through every step of developing high-quality video games using Unreal Engine and C++. From understanding the basic elements of the Unreal Editor to implementing sophisticated AI systems, the book will cover key topics through detailed explanations and hands-on projects. By the time you finish reading, you'll be capable of creating polished, professional-grade games that can stand shoulder-to-shoulder with industry-leading titles.

## Structure of the Book

The book is divided into three main sections:

1. **Beginner to Intermediate**: We start with foundational concepts in Unreal Engine and C++ programming. This section introduces you to the Unreal Editor, simple Blueprints, and beginner-friendly C++ coding tasks.
2. **Intermediate to Advanced**: We then move to more complex projects, diving deeper into C++ while focusing on real-world game scenarios such as AI behavior, physics simulations, and rendering techniques.
3. **Advanced and Expert**: Finally, we cover highly specialized topics

such as cross-platform development, multiplayer mechanics, and VR integration. Here, you'll also learn to customize the Unreal Engine source code to tailor it to your unique needs.

Throughout the book, we emphasize hands-on learning through step-by-step projects, detailed explanations, and practical exercises. By following this structured approach, you will build both your knowledge and confidence in working with C++ and Unreal Engine.

## Understanding the Audience: Who Should Read This Book

Before diving into the technical content, it's important to understand whether this book is right for you. In this section, we'll discuss the different types of readers who will benefit most from this book.

### 1. Aspiring Game Developers with Basic Programming Experience

If you have some foundational knowledge in programming (perhaps in Python, Java, or even C++ itself), this book is perfect for you. We'll start with the basics of Unreal Engine and gradually introduce C++ concepts tailored to game development. You'll get a thorough understanding of how to build functional games using Blueprints and eventually transition to coding in C++.

For example, we'll begin with simple concepts like *player movement* and *basic physics interactions*, and steadily progress to more advanced features like *AI-driven characters* and *real-time rendering*. The book's structured, project-based approach ensures that you learn the theory alongside practical applications.

### 2. Intermediate Developers Familiar with Unreal Engine or C++

If you have a working knowledge of Unreal Engine or C++, this book will help you take your skills to the next level. It's designed to deepen your understanding by diving into the intricacies of C++ code within the Unreal

Engine. We'll cover more advanced topics such as *performance optimization, multiplayer mechanics,* and *cross-platform deployment.*

For instance, we'll explore advanced character control systems, including ragdoll physics, IK solvers, and dynamic movement capabilities. This will give you a more holistic understanding of game mechanics and the interaction between C++ and Unreal's built-in systems.

## 3. Professional Developers and Indie Game Creators

If you're a professional developer or an indie creator looking to refine your skills or master Unreal Engine's advanced features, this book is packed with insights and strategies. We'll delve into engine customization, multiplayer game architecture, and even VR/AR development, providing you with the tools needed to create cutting-edge games.

You'll learn how to utilize Unreal's full capabilities to build optimized, scalable, and highly interactive games. Topics such as *networked game logic, behavior trees for AI,* and *cross-platform testing* are tailored for developers who aim to push boundaries.

## 4. Students and Educators in Game Development Programs

If you're a student studying game development, this book can be your roadmap to mastering C++ and Unreal Engine. On the other hand, if you're an educator looking for a comprehensive resource, you'll find that the book's project-based structure lends itself to course design. The blend of theory, practice, and exercises provides an effective way to help students understand complex concepts through hands-on experience.

## What to Expect

Regardless of your background, one thing remains constant: *You will be challenged.* Each chapter contains hands-on exercises and practical projects, ranging from basic mechanics to sophisticated AI systems and multiplayer setups. This book is more than a reference guide—it's a learning journey that will provide you with the technical skills and confidence to create high-quality games.

## Setting Up the Development Environment

Before embarking on this journey, it's critical to set up the right development environment. Having your tools and software correctly configured will ensure a smooth learning experience and help you focus on the core concepts without being bogged down by technical issues.

### Installing Unreal Engine

The first step is to install Unreal Engine. Unreal Engine is available for free from Epic Games' official website. You'll need to create an Epic Games account if you don't have one already. Follow these steps to get Unreal up and running on your machine:

1. **Download the Epic Games Launcher**: Go to the Unreal Engine website and download the Epic Games Launcher, which is used to manage your engine installations and projects.
2. **Install Unreal Engine**: Open the Epic Games Launcher and navigate to the *Unreal Engine* tab. From here, you can download and install the latest version of the engine.
3. **Select an Installation Directory**: During installation, choose a location on your hard drive with sufficient space (Unreal Engine installations can occupy upwards of 20GB).
4. **Launch Unreal Engine**: Once the installation is complete, open Unreal Engine from the launcher. You'll be greeted with the Unreal Project Browser, where you can create new projects or open existing ones.

## *Installing a C++ IDE (Integrated Development Environment)*

Unreal Engine uses Visual Studio as the default C++ compiler on Windows, while Xcode is the preferred choice on macOS. Setting up an IDE is essential for writing, compiling, and debugging C++ code within Unreal projects.

**Setting Up Visual Studio (Windows)**

1. **Download Visual Studio**: Visit the Microsoft Visual Studio website and download the Community edition (or a higher edition if you have a license).
2. **Install Required Components**: During installation, select the following components:

- *Desktop development with C++*: This includes necessary compilers and build tools.
- *Game Development with C++*: This includes Unreal Engine-specific integrations.

1. **Configure Visual Studio with Unreal Engine**: After installation, you may need to configure Unreal to use your Visual Studio installation. Open *Unreal Engine* and navigate to *Edit > Editor Preferences > Source Code*, then select Visual Studio from the drop-down menu.

**Setting Up Xcode (macOS)**

1. **Download Xcode**: Visit the Mac App Store and download Xcode, which is the default IDE for macOS.
2. **Install Additional Command Line Tools**: Xcode may prompt you to install additional command line tools during your first launch. Accept these prompts to install the necessary components.
3. **Configure Xcode with Unreal Engine**: Open Unreal Engine and navigate to *Edit > Editor Preferences > Source Code*, then select Xcode from the list of available IDEs.

## Creating Your First Unreal Project

Now that your software is installed, it's time to create your first Unreal project:

1. **Launch Unreal Engine**: Open the Epic Games Launcher, then launch Unreal Engine.
2. **Start a New Project**: From the Project Browser, click *New Project*.
3. **Choose a Project Template**: Unreal Engine offers several project templates such as *First Person, Third Person, Top Down,* and *Blank*. For our initial project, select *Third Person*.
4. **Select Project Settings**:

- *Blueprint vs C++*: Choose C++ as your project type to enable C++ coding features.
- *Quality Settings*: Select the *maximum quality* option if your system supports it.
- *Raytracing*: Leave this option disabled unless your hardware has the capability.

1. **Name Your Project and Set a Directory**: Give your project a descriptive name and choose a location on your hard drive. Click *Create* to generate your project files.

## Configuring Visual Studio for Unreal Development

When working with C++ in Unreal Engine, you'll be editing and debugging your code in Visual Studio. Here's how to configure Visual Studio for optimal Unreal development:

1. **Open Your Unreal Project in Visual Studio**: Right-click your Unreal project file (.uproject) and select *Generate Visual Studio project files*. Double-click the resulting .sln file to open it in Visual Studio.

2. **Configure Build Settings**: In Visual Studio, set the build configuration to *Development Editor* and the platform to *Win64* (or *Mac* if you're using Xcode). This configuration will compile your project with debugging information enabled.

3. **Building Your Project**: Click *Build > Build Solution* to compile your project. This step ensures that your code is correctly set up and ready for development.

## Understanding the Unreal Project Structure

Unreal projects are organized into a specific folder structure to help manage assets, source code, and configurations. Here's a breakdown of the main directories you'll be working with:

- **Source Folder**: Contains all your C++ source code files, including header files (.h) and implementation files (.cpp). Each class and module should have its own dedicated folder within *Source*.
- **Content Folder**: This is where all the game assets are stored, such as textures, 3D models, animations, and materials. Unreal uses a *Content Browser* to organize and access these assets.
- **Config Folder**: Stores configuration files for different aspects of your game, including input bindings, project settings, and rendering configurations.
- **Intermediate Folder**: This directory contains temporary files used during the build process. You generally don't need to modify or access these files.

## Testing Your Development Environment

With your development environment set up, it's important to test it to ensure that everything is working correctly:

1. **Open Your Project in Unreal Engine**: Launch your Unreal project

by opening the .uproject file. The Unreal Editor should load without errors.

2. **Build and Run the Project**: From the main toolbar, click *Compile* to build your project. Then click *Play* to test your game in the editor.

3. **Modify C++ Code**: Open Visual Studio and navigate to your project's *Source* folder. Open the MyCharacter.cpp file and make a small change to the character's movement speed. Save the file and recompile the project to verify that the change is reflected in the editor.

### Conclusion of the Introduction

Congratulations! You've successfully set up your development environment, created your first Unreal project, and taken the first steps towards understanding C++ in Unreal Engine. With your tools in place, you're ready to dive deeper into the world of game development.

In the upcoming chapters, we'll explore fundamental game mechanics, implement real-world gameplay features, and gradually introduce you to more advanced topics. Each chapter will build upon the last, leading you towards mastering both C++ and Unreal Engine.

By the end of this journey, you'll not only have the technical skills to create professional-quality games but also the confidence to tackle new challenges in the ever-evolving field of game development. Let's get started!

# Chapter 1: Getting Started with Unreal Engine and C++

I n this chapter, we will embark on our journey to understand Unreal Engine and its tight integration with C++. Whether you are new to Unreal or have prior experience with the basics, this chapter will guide you through setting up Unreal Engine, understanding the essentials of C++, and navigating the Unreal Editor. By the end of this chapter, you will have laid the groundwork for all future projects, setting yourself up for success in game development.

*Section 1: Installing and Configuring Unreal Engine*

### 1.1 Introduction to Unreal Engine

Before diving into installation, let's briefly discuss why Unreal Engine is such a powerful tool for game developers. Unreal Engine, developed by Epic Games, is known for its real-time 3D graphics and cutting-edge rendering capabilities. It powers some of the world's most famous video games and interactive experiences, making it the industry standard for many AAA studios and indie developers alike.

With Unreal Engine, you can create immersive environments, develop AI-driven characters, and craft engaging gameplay mechanics. And by combining it with C++, you gain complete control over game systems and the ability to fine-tune every element of your project.

**1.2 Setting Up Unreal Engine**

**1.2.1 Installing the Epic Games Launcher**

The first step to working with Unreal Engine is to install the Epic Games Launcher. The launcher serves as a hub for all Epic Games products, including Unreal Engine, and it also manages your projects, engine versions, and assets.

1. **Go to the Unreal Engine website**: Navigate to https://www.unreal engine.com and create an account if you don't have one already. This account will be used to access the launcher and download the engine.
2. **Download the Epic Games Launcher**: Click the *Download* button on the homepage to get the Epic Games Launcher installer. Once the installer is downloaded, run it and follow the on-screen instructions to complete the installation.
3. **Sign In to the Epic Games Launcher**: Open the launcher and sign in using your Epic Games account credentials.

**1.2.2 Installing Unreal Engine**

With the Epic Games Launcher installed, it's time to download and install Unreal Engine.

1. **Navigate to the Unreal Engine Tab**: In the launcher, go to the *Unreal Engine* tab on the left sidebar.
2. **Install the Latest Version**: You'll see a section for *Engine Versions*. Click on the *Install* button next to the latest available version. You can choose the installation directory if you wish to store the engine on a specific drive.
3. **Choose Components**: During installation, you can select optional components such as engine source code and additional content packs. For now, select the default options.
4. **Launch Unreal Engine**: Once installation is complete, click *Launch* to open Unreal Engine. You'll be greeted with the Project Browser, where you can create new projects or open existing ones.

## 1.3 Installing a C++ IDE (Visual Studio or Xcode)

To write and debug C++ code within Unreal Engine, you'll need an IDE. On Windows, the preferred IDE is Visual Studio, while macOS users typically use Xcode. Let's look at how to install and configure these IDEs.

### 1.3.1 Installing Visual Studio on Windows

1. **Download Visual Studio**: Go to the Visual Studio website and download the *Community Edition* if you don't have a paid license. The Community Edition is free and sufficient for Unreal Engine development.
2. **Select the Required Components**: During installation, select the following components:

* *Desktop development with C++*: Includes essential build tools and libraries.
* *Game development with C++*: Integrates Visual Studio with Unreal Engine.

1. **Complete the Installation**: Follow the prompts to install Visual Studio. Once installed, open Visual Studio and complete any initial configuration.

### 1.3.2 Installing Xcode on macOS

1. **Download Xcode**: Visit the Mac App Store and search for *Xcode*. Download and install Xcode on your macOS device.
2. **Install Command Line Tools**: Xcode may prompt you to install additional command line tools during its first launch. Accept these prompts to install the necessary components.
3. **Configure Xcode with Unreal Engine**: In Unreal Engine, navigate to *Edit > Editor Preferences > Source Code*, and select Xcode from the dropdown menu.

## 1.4 Creating a New Unreal Project

Now that Unreal Engine and your IDE are set up, it's time to create your first Unreal project. We will create a simple project using the *Third Person* template.

1. **Open the Project Browser**: When you launch Unreal Engine, the Project Browser appears. Click on *New Project* to create a new project.
2. **Select a Template**: Choose *Third Person* from the list of available templates. This template provides a character with basic movement controls.
3. **Select C++ as the Project Type**: Choose *C++* as the project type to enable C++ coding features within your project.
4. **Configure Project Settings**:

- *Name your project*: Give your project a descriptive name, such as *MyFirstProject*.
- *Select quality and target hardware*: Choose *Maximum Quality* and *Desktop/-Console* for your initial project.

1. **Create the Project**: Click *Create* to generate your new project files. Unreal Engine will load your project and take you to the editor's main interface.

## Section 2: C++ Essentials for Unreal Development

To work effectively with Unreal Engine, you need to understand the essentials of C++. While Unreal Engine offers Blueprints for visual scripting, using C++ allows for deeper customization, improved performance, and more efficient memory management.

### 2.1 C++ Basics Refresher

Before diving into Unreal-specific C++ topics, let's briefly review some fundamental concepts in C++. These concepts will be crucial as you start developing your game.

- **Variables and Data Types**: In C++, variables are used to store information. There are several fundamental data types, such as int, float, double, char, and bool. Unreal also offers specialized data types, such as FVector (for storing 3D vectors).

```cpp
Copy code
int Health = 100; // An integer variable
float Speed = 600.0f; // A floating-point variable
FVector Position(0.0f, 0.0f, 0.0f); // A 3D vector using Unreal's
FVector
```

- **Control Structures**: C++ supports common control structures like if, for, while, and switch. These structures allow you to implement conditional logic and loops.

```cpp
Copy code
if (Health <= 0)
{
    // Handle player death
}
```

- **Functions**: Functions allow you to encapsulate logic that you can call from other parts of your code. In Unreal, functions are often used to define game mechanics and interactions.

```cpp
Copy code
void TakeDamage(int DamageAmount)
{
    Health -= DamageAmount;
```

```
    if (Health <= 0)
    {
        // Trigger player death logic
    }
}
```

- **Object-Oriented Programming**: C++ is an object-oriented language, which means it supports classes and objects. In Unreal, almost everything is represented as a class, such as ACharacter, APlayerController, or UObject.

## 2.2 Understanding Unreal's Class Structure

Unreal Engine organizes code through a class hierarchy. Most gameplay classes inherit from AActor or UObject. Here's a quick rundown of some of the most common classes:

- **AActor**: Represents any object that can exist in the game world. Examples include characters, pickups, weapons, and vehicles.
- **ACharacter**: A specialized subclass of AActor that provides built-in movement and animation controls for player characters.
- **UObject**: The base class for all objects that aren't directly placed in the world. Unreal uses UObjects to manage in-game assets, data containers, and game systems.

## 2.3 Creating Your First C++ Class

Let's create a simple C++ class within Unreal Engine to demonstrate how C++ interacts with the engine.

1. **Open Your Project in Unreal**: Make sure your project is open in Unreal Engine.
2. **Create a New C++ Class**: In the Content Browser, click on *Add New > C++ Class*. Select Actor as the parent class, since AActor is the base class

16

for all in-game objects.

3. **Name Your Class**: Give your class a descriptive name, such as *MyActorClass*, and click *Create Class*. Unreal will automatically generate the header (.h) and implementation (.cpp) files for your new class.

4. **Open Your C++ Class in Visual Studio**: Navigate to the *Source* folder in Visual Studio and open MyActorClass.cpp. You'll see a basic class definition similar to the following:

```cpp
Copy code
#include "MyActorClass.h"

AMyActorClass::AMyActorClass()
{
    PrimaryActorTick.bCanEverTick = true;
}

void AMyActorClass::BeginPlay()
{
    Super::BeginPlay();
}

void AMyActorClass::Tick(float DeltaTime)
{
    Super::Tick(DeltaTime);
}
```

## 2.4 Understanding Header and Source Files

C++ classes in Unreal are split into two files: a header file (.h) and a source file (.cpp). The header file contains the class definition, including member variables and function declarations, while the source file contains the actual function implementations.

For example, in MyActorClass.h, you might define a variable and a function like this:

```
cpp
Copy code
public:
    int32 Health; // A public variable to store health

    // A function declaration
    void TakeDamage(int32 DamageAmount);
```

In MyActorClass.cpp, you would provide the implementation for the TakeDamage function:

```
cpp
Copy code
void AMyActorClass::TakeDamage(int32 DamageAmount)
{
    Health -= DamageAmount;
    if (Health <= 0)
    {
        // Handle actor destruction or game over logic
    }
}
```

Understanding this structure is critical for working with Unreal Engine, as it forms the backbone of how you'll organize your game code.

## Section 3: Navigating the Unreal Editor

The Unreal Editor is the heart of your game development workflow. It's where you'll spend most of your time creating levels, placing actors, and building gameplay features. In this section, we'll explore the key components of the editor and show you how to navigate its interface efficiently.

### 3.1 The Main Interface

When you open a project in Unreal Engine, you're greeted with the main interface. This interface is divided into several key panels:

1. **Viewport**: The Viewport is where you can view and interact with your

game world. You can move around the scene using the WASD keys or by holding down the right mouse button.

2. **Content Browser**: The Content Browser is the central hub for managing your game's assets. It's where you'll find textures, materials, meshes, and more.

3. **Details Panel**: When you select an object in the Viewport, the Details Panel shows all of its properties. You can modify an object's appearance, behavior, and transform values here.

4. **Modes Panel**: This panel contains tools for placing objects, editing geometry, and creating landscapes. The default mode is *Place Mode*, which allows you to drag and drop actors into the world.

### 3.2 Working with Actors

In Unreal, an *Actor* is any object that exists in the game world. This could be a static mesh, a light source, or a player character. Here's how to work with actors in the editor:

1. **Placing Actors**: To place an actor, drag and drop it from the Modes Panel into the Viewport. For example, drag a *Cube* object into the scene.

2. **Transforming Actors**: Use the *Move, Rotate*, and *Scale* tools to adjust an actor's position, rotation, and size. You can switch between these tools using the keyboard shortcuts W, E, and R.

3. **Editing Actor Properties**: Select an actor and view its properties in the Details Panel. Here, you can change its material, set physics options, or adjust collision settings.

### 3.3 Building a Simple Level

Let's create a simple level to get a feel for how the editor works:

1. **Create a New Level**: In the *File* menu, select *New Level* and choose *Default Level*. This level will include a basic ground plane and a light source.

2. **Add Static Meshes**: Drag a *Cube* and a *Sphere* from the Modes Panel

into the Viewport. Arrange them to create a basic obstacle course.

3. **Add a Player Start**: From the Modes Panel, drag a *Player Start* actor into the level. This will define where the player character spawns.

4. **Test the Level**: Click *Play* to enter the game and test your level. Use the WASD keys to move your character around.

## 3.4 Saving and Managing Projects

It's essential to save your work regularly to avoid losing progress. Here's how to manage your projects effectively:

1. **Save Levels**: Go to *File > Save Current Level* to save your active level. It's a good idea to save multiple versions of your level as you make significant changes.

2. **Save All**: To save all assets and configurations, click *Save All* from the main toolbar. This will save your level, project settings, and content files.

3. **Managing Projects**: The Epic Games Launcher allows you to manage multiple projects. Use the *Library* tab to view and open all of your Unreal projects.

## 3.5 Tips for Efficient Navigation

- **Use Keyboard Shortcuts**: Learning keyboard shortcuts can save you a lot of time. For example, press F to focus on a selected actor in the Viewport.
- **Duplicate Actors Quickly**: To quickly duplicate an actor, hold down the Alt key and drag the actor in the Viewport.
- **Organize Your Content Browser**: Create folders in the Content Browser to organize your assets by type, such as *Textures*, *Meshes*, and *Blueprints*.

## Conclusion of Chapter 1

Congratulations on completing Chapter 1! You've successfully set up Unreal Engine, learned the essentials of C++, and familiarized yourself with the Unreal Editor. These foundational skills will be crucial as you progress through the book and start building more complex game features.

In the next chapter, we'll dive deeper into Blueprints and explore how to integrate them with C++ for efficient and versatile game development. You'll also start building your first game project, putting all of your newly acquired skills to the test.

# Chapter 2: Unreal Blueprints and C++ Integration

I n the previous chapter, we laid the groundwork for understanding Unreal Engine and the essentials of C++ within the Unreal framework. Now, it's time to explore one of the most powerful features of Unreal Engine: Blueprints. We will discuss what Blueprints are, how to create and manipulate them, and more importantly, how to effectively integrate Blueprints and C++ to create a flexible and high-performance game project. By the end of this chapter, you'll have a solid grasp of both Blueprints and C++ integration, allowing you to leverage the best of both worlds.

## Section 1: Introduction to Unreal Blueprints

### 1.1 What Are Blueprints?

Blueprints are Unreal Engine's visual scripting language. They allow you to define and create gameplay elements, interactions, and events without writing code. Essentially, Blueprints provide a graphical interface for programming logic, making them accessible to non-programmers while still maintaining robust functionality for developers familiar with code. Blueprints are powerful enough to handle complex logic but are also highly intuitive for designers and artists.

While C++ offers greater control and performance optimization, Blueprints enable quick prototyping and implementation. A well-rounded game developer will be comfortable working in both C++ and Blueprints, seamlessly blending the two for the best results.

## 1.2 Types of Blueprints

Unreal Engine offers several types of Blueprints, each serving different purposes:

1. **Actor Blueprints**: Used to define the behavior of in-game objects or actors, such as characters, weapons, or interactable items.
2. **Level Blueprints**: Specific to the current level, Level Blueprints handle level-specific events, interactions, and logic.
3. **Widget Blueprints**: Primarily used for creating user interfaces (UIs) within the game. Widget Blueprints enable the creation of buttons, HUDs, and menus.
4. **Function and Macro Libraries**: Collections of reusable functions or macros that can be used across multiple Blueprints.

## 1.3 When to Use Blueprints and When to Use C++

It's crucial to understand when to use Blueprints versus C++. Blueprints are ideal for quick iterations, prototyping, and setting up simple gameplay interactions. C++ is recommended for performance-critical elements, complex systems, and when detailed control over memory and processing is required.

**Blueprints:**

- **Prototyping and Iteration**: Create and test gameplay ideas quickly.
- **Simple Interactions**: Set up basic player controls, triggers, and environmental effects.
- **UI Elements**: Build UI elements like health bars, inventory menus, and pop-up messages.

C++:

- **Performance Optimization**: Handle performance-heavy calculations and functions.
- **Advanced Systems**: Implement advanced AI behaviors, networking logic, or custom physics.
- **Custom Actor Classes**: Define complex game objects with intricate interactions.

## Section 2: Creating and Working with Blueprints

### 2.1 Creating a Simple Blueprint

To better understand Blueprints, let's create a simple Blueprint class for a basic pickup item.

1. **Open Your Project**: Make sure you have an active project open in Unreal Engine.
2. **Create a New Blueprint Class**: In the Content Browser, click *Add New* and select *Blueprint Class*. Choose *Actor* as the base class, as it represents in-game objects.
3. **Name Your Blueprint**: Name it *BP_Pickup*.
4. **Adding Components**: Double-click the new Blueprint to open it in the Blueprint Editor. From the *Components* tab, add a *Static Mesh Component* to represent the visual aspect of the pickup. Select an appropriate mesh, such as a sphere or cube.
5. **Setting Properties**: In the Details panel, adjust the size, scale, and collision properties of the Static Mesh. Set the collision to "Overlap" so it can trigger events when a player touches it.

### 2.2 Adding Blueprint Logic

1. **Adding a Collision Event**: Select the Static Mesh component and scroll down to the *Events* section in the Details panel. Click *OnComponentBegi*

*nOverlap* to create a new event node in the Event Graph.

2. **Adding Logic**: From the event node, create a sequence of nodes that add points to the player's score and then destroy the pickup item. Use nodes like *Get Player Character*, *Cast to MyCharacter*, *Add Score*, and *Destroy Actor*.

### 2.3 Testing the Blueprint

1. **Place the Pickup in the Level**: Return to your level, drag and drop the *BP_Pickup* Blueprint into the scene. Place multiple instances to create a simple collectible system.
2. **Play the Game**: Click *Play* to enter the game and test the Blueprint functionality. Check that the pickups are destroyed upon overlap and that the player's score increases.

## 2.4 Debugging Blueprints

Unreal Engine provides built-in tools to debug Blueprints. While testing, you can:

- **Watch Variable Values**: Right-click on a variable in the Blueprint and select *Watch This Variable* to monitor its value during gameplay.
- **Use Breakpoints**: Right-click on a node and select *Add Breakpoint*. When the node is executed, the game will pause, allowing you to inspect the state of your variables and actors.

## Section 3: Integrating C++ and Blueprints

### 3.1 Exposing C++ Functions to Blueprints

One of the best features of Unreal Engine is the ability to create functions in C++ and expose them to Blueprints. This enables you to use C++ for performance-intensive tasks while leveraging Blueprints for high-level logic and quick iterations.

**Creating a C++ Function and Exposing It to Blueprints**

1. **Open Your C++ Class**: In Visual Studio, open your project and navigate to your custom C++ class (e.g., MyCharacter.cpp).
2. **Declare the Function in the Header File**: In MyCharacter.h, declare a function with the UFUNCTION macro to expose it to Blueprints:

```cpp
Copy code
UFUNCTION(BlueprintCallable, Category = "Gameplay")
void AddScore(int32 Points);
```

1. **Define the Function in the Source File**: In MyCharacter.cpp, define the function:

```cpp
Copy code
void AMyCharacter::AddScore(int32 Points)
{
    PlayerScore += Points;
}
```

1. **Calling the Function in a Blueprint**: In the Blueprint Editor, select *MyCharacter* and drag out a node. You should see the AddScore function available under *Gameplay*. This function can now be called from within Blueprints.

**3.2 Creating Blueprint Variables in C++**

To make a C++ variable editable in Blueprints, use the UPROPERTY macro. This allows you to modify variables directly from the Blueprint Editor.

1. **Declare the Variable in the Header File**: Add the following line to MyCharacter.h:

```cpp
Copy code
UPROPERTY(EditAnywhere, BlueprintReadWrite, Category = "Gameplay")
int32 PlayerScore;
```

1. **Accessing and Modifying Variables in Blueprints**: You can now access and modify PlayerScore directly from Blueprints. For example, you can add nodes that increase the score when the player collects pickups or completes objectives.

### 3.3 Extending Blueprints with C++

In some cases, you may want to create a custom C++ class that serves as the base class for a Blueprint. This allows you to define core logic in C++ while giving designers the flexibility to build and modify content in Blueprints.

1. **Create a Custom C++ Class**: In Unreal Engine, create a new C++ class derived from Actor. Name it *CustomPickup*.
2. **Define Basic Functionality in C++**: Add basic functionality in C++ to handle collisions and pickup logic:

```cpp
Copy code
// In CustomPickup.h
UPROPERTY(EditAnywhere, BlueprintReadWrite, Category = "Pickup")
bool bIsCollected;

// In CustomPickup.cpp
ACustomPickup::ACustomPickup()
{
```

```
    // Set default value
    bIsCollected = false;
}
```

1. **Create a Blueprint Derived from the C++ Class**: In the Content Browser, right-click on *CustomPickup* and choose *Create Blueprint Based on This Class*. This new Blueprint can now utilize all of the C++ functionality while allowing you to add additional components or tweak properties.

## Section 4: Real-World Use Cases of C++ and Blueprints

### 4.1 Character Abilities and Power-ups

For example, you might want to implement special abilities or power-ups that your character can collect and activate. Here's how you can handle this using C++ for core functionality and Blueprints for variations:

1. **Define the Base Ability in C++**: Create a base class in C++ that handles core ability logic such as cooldowns, duration, and activation effects.
2. **Derive Specific Abilities in Blueprints**: Create a Blueprint class for each ability, tweaking parameters like cooldown time, visual effects, and damage multipliers.

### 4.2 AI Behavior with Behavior Trees and C++

While Unreal's Behavior Tree system is heavily based on Blueprints, you can extend its capabilities using C++. For instance, you might want to implement custom decorators or services in C++ to handle more complex decision-making logic.

1. **Create a C++ Class for a Custom AI Task**: Create a new C++ class derived from BTTaskNode. Implement custom logic for AI behaviors like seeking cover, flanking, or using special abilities.

2. **Expose the Custom Task to Blueprints**: Use the UCLASS and UFUNCTION macros to expose your custom task, allowing it to be utilized within the Behavior Tree Editor.

### 4.3 UI Elements and Player Feedback

When creating UI elements such as health bars, inventory menus, or dialogue systems, it's often more efficient to define the core logic in C++ and use Widget Blueprints to build the actual UI.

1. **Define UI Logic in C++**: Create a C++ class that handles UI events, such as updating health values or triggering notifications.
2. **Create Widget Blueprints**: Build the visual elements of the UI using Widget Blueprints. Use Blueprint nodes to bind the visual elements to your C++ class functions and variables.

## Section 5: Advanced Techniques for Blueprint and C++ Integration

### 5.1 Creating Custom Blueprint Nodes

Sometimes, the built-in Blueprint nodes may not be sufficient for your needs. In these cases, you can create custom Blueprint nodes in C++ using the K2Node class.

1. **Create a Custom Blueprint Node Class**: In Visual Studio, create a new C++ class derived from K2Node.
2. **Implement Node Logic**: Define the logic for your custom node in the source file. This could include calculations, event handling, or interacting with other actors.
3. **Register the Node in the Editor**: Once your node is complete, register it in Unreal Editor so it appears in the Blueprint node search.

### 5.2 Extending Gameplay Framework Classes

Unreal Engine provides several built-in gameplay classes, such as ACharacter, APlayerController, and AGameMode. By extending these classes in C++, you can create new gameplay mechanics and rules.

1. **Creating a Custom Game Mode**: Extend AGameMode in C++ to define new game rules, such as win conditions, respawn mechanics, or custom scoring.
2. **Integrating with Blueprints**: Expose key variables and functions from your custom Game Mode class to Blueprints, allowing you to create dynamic in-game events and adjust settings without modifying C++ code.

## Conclusion of Chapter 2

In this chapter, we explored the power of Unreal Engine's Blueprints and learned how to integrate them seamlessly with C++. You've seen how Blueprints can be used for rapid prototyping and creating gameplay interactions, while C++ allows for greater control and optimization. By understanding the strengths of each, you can decide when to use Blueprints and when to dive into C++ to achieve the best results.

From creating simple pickups to building advanced AI and UI systems, you've gained practical experience working with Blueprints and C++ in tandem. As you continue through the book, you'll be building on this foundation to create more complex and interactive gameplay experiences.

In the next chapter, we will dive deeper into the creation of interactive 3D environments, focusing on level design, lighting, and visual effects. Stay tuned as we continue our journey to mastering game development with C++ and Unreal Engine.

# Chapter 3: Building and Customizing Interactive 3D Environments

C reating visually stunning and interactive 3D environments is one of the hallmarks of high-quality game development. Unreal Engine is packed with powerful tools and features that allow you to design, build, and customize immersive worlds. In this chapter, we will cover everything you need to know about building dynamic environments, implementing advanced lighting techniques, and using Unreal's built-in systems to create realistic effects and materials.

By the end of this chapter, you will have a solid understanding of environment design principles and practical knowledge of Unreal's tools to build levels, apply realistic materials, and integrate interactivity into your game world.

## Section 1: Designing and Building Levels in Unreal Engine

### 1.1 Understanding Level Design Basics

Level design is the process of creating the structure and layout of a game environment. It involves defining spaces, obstacles, points of interest, and visual elements that guide the player through a cohesive experience. A good level design not only looks appealing but also enhances gameplay by providing intuitive pathways, creating challenges, and establishing mood through environmental storytelling.

**Key Principles of Level Design**:

- **Visual Hierarchy**: Use lighting, colors, and visual elements to draw the player's attention to key areas.
- **Navigation and Flow**: Design the layout to guide players smoothly from one point to another.
- **Gameplay Integration**: Integrate challenges, puzzles, and interactions that align with the game's core mechanics.
- **Balancing Detail and Space**: Balance areas of high visual detail with open spaces to avoid overwhelming the player.

## 1.2 Getting Started with the Level Editor

Unreal Engine's Level Editor is your primary workspace for building and modifying game environments. Let's get familiar with the Level Editor interface and its core components.

**1.2.1 The Viewport and Navigation**: The Viewport is where you'll create and manipulate your 3D environment. You can move around the Viewport using the WASD keys or by holding down the right mouse button while dragging the mouse.

**1.2.2 Modes Panel**: The Modes Panel allows you to switch between different tools for placing and modifying actors, geometry, and landscapes. The most commonly used modes are:

- **Place Mode**: For placing static meshes, lights, cameras, and other actors.
- **Geometry Editing Mode**: For modifying basic shapes and geometry.
- **Landscape Mode**: For creating and sculpting landscapes and terrain.

## 1.3 Building Basic Level Geometry

To create a basic level, you'll need to start by laying out the foundational geometry using static meshes and shapes.

1. **Placing Basic Shapes**: Go to the Modes Panel and drag basic shapes

(like a cube, sphere, or cylinder) into the Viewport. These shapes can be used to create the layout of rooms, platforms, and barriers.

2. **Manipulating Shapes**: Use the *Move, Rotate*, and *Scale* tools (keyboard shortcuts: W, E, and R) to arrange and resize the shapes as needed. Combine multiple shapes to create larger structures.

3. **Using BSP Brushes**: BSP (Binary Space Partitioning) brushes are a quick way to block out level geometry. Drag a BSP box into the scene and use the Details Panel to adjust its dimensions. BSP brushes can be converted into static meshes later in the development process.

### 1.4 Creating and Modifying Terrain with the Landscape Tool

The Landscape Tool in Unreal Engine allows you to create large outdoor environments with hills, valleys, rivers, and more.

1. **Creating a New Landscape**: Go to the Modes Panel and select *Landscape*. In the Landscape Tool settings, choose a suitable size and resolution for your landscape. Click *Create* to add the landscape to your level.

2. **Sculpting the Terrain**: Use the *Sculpt* tool to raise or lower parts of the landscape. You can adjust the brush size and strength to control the terrain's shape and smoothness. Combine different brushes to create diverse terrain features.

3. **Painting Textures on the Landscape**: Once your terrain is sculpted, switch to the *Paint* mode to apply different textures to your landscape. You can create materials that blend between different textures, such as grass, dirt, and rocks.

### 1.5 Placing Static Meshes and Props

Static meshes are 3D models that represent objects and structures in your level. These can range from simple props to detailed buildings and vehicles.

1. **Adding Static Meshes**: Drag a static mesh from the Content Browser into the Viewport. Common examples include crates, walls, trees, and

furniture.

2. **Setting Up Collision for Static Meshes**: To make sure that players and other objects can interact with a static mesh, you need to set up its collision properties. Select the static mesh and open its details to adjust collision settings.

## Section 2: Lighting and Shadows in Unreal Engine

### 2.1 Introduction to Lighting Concepts

Lighting is one of the most crucial elements in creating an immersive and visually compelling environment. In Unreal Engine, you have access to several types of lights and advanced lighting features that enable you to achieve realistic results.

**Basic Lighting Types**:

- **Directional Light**: Simulates sunlight or moonlight, affecting all objects in the scene uniformly.
- **Point Light**: Emits light in all directions from a single point, similar to a light bulb.
- **Spot Light**: Emits a cone-shaped beam of light, perfect for simulating flashlights or stage lights.
- **Rect Light**: Used for more controlled lighting, like TV screens or windows.

### 2.2 Setting Up Basic Lighting

1. **Adding a Directional Light**: Go to the Modes Panel and drag a Directional Light into the Viewport. This light simulates sunlight and can be adjusted to create different times of day.
2. **Adjusting Light Properties**: Select the Directional Light and open the Details Panel. Here, you can adjust properties such as intensity, color, and rotation.
3. **Adding Point and Spot Lights**: Place Point and Spot Lights to highlight

specific areas of your level. For example, use Point Lights to illuminate rooms and Spot Lights to create dramatic lighting effects.

## 2.3 Advanced Lighting Techniques

1. **Global Illumination and Lightmass**: Global Illumination (GI) calculates how light bounces off surfaces, creating realistic ambient lighting. Unreal Engine uses Lightmass for static GI calculations. To bake lighting, go to *Build > Lighting Only*.
2. **Using Light Channels**: Light Channels allow you to control which lights affect which objects. For instance, you can create a specific light for a character's weapon that doesn't affect the rest of the environment.
3. **Volumetric Fog**: Volumetric Fog is a technique for creating realistic fog effects that interact with lighting. Enable Volumetric Fog in the fog actor's settings to simulate foggy environments or dramatic shafts of light.

## 2.4 Realistic Shadows and Reflections

1. **Dynamic Shadows**: Unreal Engine supports real-time dynamic shadows for moving objects. Adjust the shadow settings in the light source's properties to control shadow resolution and softness.
2. **Planar Reflections and Screen Space Reflections**: Use Planar Reflections for perfect reflections on flat surfaces like mirrors or water. For dynamic reflections on more complex surfaces, enable Screen Space Reflections (SSR) in the post-processing volume.

## Section 3: Materials and Textures

### 3.1 Introduction to Materials

Materials define how surfaces interact with light, determining an object's color, shininess, roughness, and more. Unreal Engine uses a node-based Material Editor that allows you to create custom materials with ease.

**Key Material Properties**:

- **Base Color**: The primary color of the material.
- **Roughness**: Controls the sharpness of reflections. Low roughness values create shiny surfaces, while high roughness values create matte surfaces.
- **Metallic**: Determines whether the surface behaves like a metal.
- **Normal Map**: Adds fine surface details such as bumps and scratches without affecting the mesh's geometry.

## 3.2 Creating a Simple Material

1. **Open the Material Editor**: In the Content Browser, right-click and select *Material*. Name the new material *M_BasicMaterial*. Double-click to open the Material Editor.
2. **Adding Nodes**: In the Material Editor, you'll see a graph with a node representing the output material. Add a *Constant3Vector* node to define the base color and connect it to the *Base Color* input.
3. **Adjusting Roughness and Metallic Properties**: Add *Constant* nodes for roughness and metallic values. Connect these nodes to the corresponding inputs in the material node.

## 3.3 Creating Complex Materials with Multiple Textures

1. **Using Texture Maps**: Import a texture into the Content Browser, then open your material in the Material Editor. Add a *Texture Sample* node and select your imported texture. Connect it to the *Base Color* input.
2. **Blending Textures**: Add multiple texture samples to create more detailed materials. Use a *Lerp* (Linear Interpolation) node to blend between textures based on a mask or vertex color.
3. **Adding Normal and Specular Maps**: Connect normal and specular maps to their respective inputs to create detailed surfaces with reflections and fine details.

## Section 4: Creating Dynamic and Interactive Environments

### 4.1 Introduction to Blueprint Visual Scripting for Interactivity

While C++ gives you full control over game logic, Blueprints are ideal for adding dynamic elements and interactions to your environment. Let's explore some common uses for Blueprints in level design.

**Common Uses for Blueprints:**

- **Trigger Volumes**: Create areas that activate events when the player enters them, such as opening doors or starting cutscenes.
- **Movable Platforms**: Set up platforms that move when a button is pressed or a lever is pulled.
- **Environmental Hazards**: Add traps, obstacles, and other dangers that challenge the player.

### 4.2 Creating a Simple Door Blueprint

1. **Creating a New Blueprint Class**: Create a new Blueprint class derived from *Actor* and name it *BP_Door*.
2. **Adding Components**: Add a Static Mesh Component to represent the door. In the *Components* tab, add a Box Collision component around the door to act as the trigger volume.
3. **Adding Logic**: In the Event Graph, add an *OnComponentBeginOverlap* event for the Box Collision. Create logic to rotate or slide the door open when the player enters the collision volume.
4. **3 Setting Up Movable Platforms**
5. **Creating a Platform Blueprint**: Create a new Blueprint class derived from *Actor* and name it *BP_Platform*. Add a Static Mesh Component to represent the platform.
6. **Adding Movement Logic**: In the Event Graph, use a *Timeline* node to animate the platform's movement. Connect the Timeline's output to the platform's position using a *Set Actor Location* node.
7. **Triggering the Platform**: Add a Trigger Volume to the level and create

logic to activate the platform's movement when the player steps onto the trigger.

## 4.4 Building Dynamic Environmental Effects

1. **Using Particle Systems for Visual Effects**: Unreal Engine includes a powerful particle editor called *Niagara*. Create a new particle system and use it to generate visual effects such as smoke, fire, or water splashes.
2. **Applying Audio to Enhance Immersion**: Add audio components to your Blueprints to play sounds when events occur. For example, play a creaking sound when a door opens or a splash sound when the player enters water.

## Section 5: Level Optimization Techniques

### 5.1 Level Streaming and Optimization

As your levels become more complex, you'll need to manage their performance to ensure smooth gameplay. Unreal Engine offers several optimization techniques to help with this.

1. **Using Level Streaming**: Divide large levels into smaller sections called sub-levels. Load and unload these sub-levels dynamically based on the player's location to save memory and processing power.
2. **Culling and LOD (Level of Detail)**: Use culling to hide objects that are far away from the player. Implement LODs for meshes to automatically switch to lower-resolution versions when the player is far away.

### 5.2 Optimizing Lighting and Shadows

1. **Using Static and Stationary Lights**: Use static lights for objects that never move to reduce the computational cost. Stationary lights offer a balance between dynamic lighting and baked lighting.
2. **Reducing Shadow Complexity**: Limit the number of dynamic shad-

ows or adjust shadow quality settings to improve performance on lower-end systems.

## Conclusion of Chapter 3

Congratulations! You've completed Chapter 3, which covered the essential tools and techniques for building interactive 3D environments in Unreal Engine. You've learned how to design levels, create and manipulate terrain, set up realistic lighting, and use materials and textures to enhance the visual appeal of your game world. Moreover, you've explored how to add dynamic elements and interactions to your environment using Blueprints, and you've learned how to optimize your levels for performance.

With this foundation in place, you're ready to move on to more advanced gameplay mechanics and AI systems in the following chapters. Your journey to mastering Unreal Engine and C++ is progressing well, and the skills you've learned in this chapter will serve as a cornerstone for the rest of the book.

# Chapter 4: Developing Advanced Gameplay Mechanics with C++

I n game development, crafting engaging and memorable gameplay mechanics is crucial to building a successful game. Unreal Engine offers extensive tools and systems to develop advanced gameplay elements, but understanding how to implement them effectively in C++ is key to creating a polished game. In this chapter, we will explore how to build and customize various gameplay mechanics using C++. We'll cover topics such as implementing complex character controls, developing robust AI systems, creating custom camera systems, and integrating physics-based interactions.

By the end of this chapter, you'll be equipped with the skills to design and implement advanced gameplay mechanics, enhancing the interactivity and depth of your game.

## Section 1: Advanced Character Controls and Movement Systems

### 1.1 Implementing Complex Character Movement

One of the most critical aspects of creating engaging gameplay is ensuring that your character's movement feels smooth and responsive. Unreal Engine provides built-in movement components, but to stand out, you may want to implement more sophisticated mechanics.

**Key Character Movement Types**:

- **Sprinting**: Allow the player to move at a faster speed when holding down a button.
- **Crouching**: Enable the player to lower their character's height for stealth or accessing low spaces.
- **Wall Jumping**: Implement a mechanic that lets the player jump off walls to reach higher areas.
- **Dashing and Rolling**: Add quick bursts of movement to dodge attacks or traverse the environment rapidly.

## 1.2 Creating a Custom Character Class in C++

1. **Extending the Character Class**: Create a new C++ class derived from ACharacter. Name this class *AdvancedCharacter*.
2. **Defining Movement States**: In the header file (AdvancedCharacter.h), define variables for movement states such as sprinting, crouching, and dashing:

```cpp
Copy code
UPROPERTY(EditAnywhere, BlueprintReadWrite, Category = "Movement")
bool bIsSprinting;

UPROPERTY(EditAnywhere, BlueprintReadWrite, Category = "Movement")
bool bIsCrouching;
```

1. **Implementing Movement Functions**: In the source file (AdvancedCharacter.cpp), implement functions to handle state changes:

```cpp
Copy code
```

41

```
void AAdvancedCharacter::StartSprint()
{
    bIsSprinting = true;
    GetCharacterMovement()->MaxWalkSpeed *= 2.0f; // Double the
    walk speed
}

void AAdvancedCharacter::StopSprint()
{
    bIsSprinting = false;
    GetCharacterMovement()->MaxWalkSpeed /= 2.0f; // Restore
    original speed
}

void AAdvancedCharacter::ToggleCrouch()
{
    bIsCrouching = !bIsCrouching;
    Crouch(bIsCrouching); // Toggle crouch state
}
```

## 1.3 Implementing Double Jump and Wall Jump

1. **Double Jump Mechanic:** In the character class, override the Jump function to allow a second jump while airborne:

```cpp
Copy code
void AAdvancedCharacter::Jump()
{
    if (CanJump())
    {
        Super::Jump();
        JumpCounter++;
    }
    else if (JumpCounter < MaxDoubleJumpCount)
    {
```

```
        LaunchCharacter(FVector(0.0f, 0.0f, DoubleJumpHeight),
        false, true);
        JumpCounter++;
    }
}
```

1. **Wall Jump Mechanic**: Use a line trace to detect walls and allow the player to jump off them:

```cpp
Copy code
void AAdvancedCharacter::PerformWallJump()
{
    FVector WallNormal;
    if (DetectWall(WallNormal))
    {
        FVector JumpDirection = WallNormal + FVector::UpVector;
        LaunchCharacter(JumpDirection * WallJumpStrength, true,
        true);
    }
}

bool AAdvancedCharacter::DetectWall(FVector& OutWallNormal)
{
    // Implement a line trace here to detect walls and return true
    if a wall is found
}
```

## 1.4 Adding Animations for Advanced Movement

Animations can enhance the realism of your character's movement. Create animation states and transitions for actions like sprinting, crouching, and jumping.

1. **Setting Up an Animation Blueprint**: Open the Animation Blueprint for your character and create new states for each movement type (e.g.,

43

Sprint, Crouch, Jump).

2. **Adding Blend Spaces**: Use Blend Spaces to smoothly transition between different movement animations based on the character's speed and direction.

3. **Triggering Animations in C++**: In your character class, update the Animation Blueprint's state variables in response to input or events:

```cpp
Copy code
void AAdvancedCharacter::UpdateAnimationState()
{
    if (bIsSprinting)
    {
        // Trigger sprint animation state
    }
    else if (bIsCrouching)
    {
        // Trigger crouch animation state
    }
}
```

## Section 2: Developing AI Behavior Systems with C++

### 2.1 Understanding Unreal Engine's AI Framework

Unreal Engine offers powerful AI systems, including behavior trees, blackboards, and nav meshes. While much of the AI setup can be done using Blueprints, C++ allows you to create custom tasks, services, and decorators to achieve more advanced AI behaviors.

**Key AI Components**:

- **Behavior Trees**: Graphs that define AI decision-making logic.
- **Blackboards**: Data containers for AI variables, shared across tasks.
- **Navigation Meshes**: Areas that define where AI characters can move.

## 2.2 Creating a Custom AI Controller in C++

1. **Extending the AIController Class**: Create a new C++ class derived from AAIController. Name this class *CustomAIController*.
2. **Setting Up the AI Controller**: In the header file, declare a function to possess an AI character and initialize the Blackboard and Behavior Tree:

```cpp
Copy code
UPROPERTY(EditAnywhere, Category = "AI")
UBehaviorTree* AIBehaviorTree;

UPROPERTY(EditAnywhere, Category = "AI")
UBlackboardComponent* AIBlackboard;
```

1. **Implementing AI Possession Logic**: In the source file, implement the Possess function:

```cpp
Copy code
void ACustomAIController::Possess(APawn* InPawn)
{
    Super::Possess(InPawn);
    if (AIBehaviorTree)
    {
        RunBehaviorTree(AIBehaviorTree);
    }
}
```

## 2.3 Creating Custom AI Tasks in C++

1. **Creating a Task Class**: Create a new C++ class derived from UBTTaskNode. Name it *FindCoverTask*.

45

2. **Defining Task Logic**: Override the ExecuteTask function to find a nearby cover location:

```cpp
Copy code
EBTNodeResult::Type
UFindCoverTask::ExecuteTask(UBehaviorTreeComponent& OwnerComp,
uint8* NodeMemory)
{
    // Logic to find cover and move AI character
}
```

1. **Exposing the Task to Blueprints**: Use the UCLASS and UFUNCTION macros to expose the task to the Behavior Tree Editor.

### 2.4 Implementing Perception Systems and AI Senses

1. **Setting Up AI Perception**: Create a new component in your AI character class called UAIPerceptionComponent. Add AI senses such as sight and hearing.
2. **Handling AI Perception Events**: Override the OnPerceptionUpdated function to respond to stimuli:

```cpp
Copy code
void ACustomAIController::OnPerceptionUpdated(const
TArray<AActor*>& UpdatedActors)
{
    // Logic to handle when the AI sees or hears something
}
```

## *Section 3: Implementing Camera Systems and Player Views*

### 3.1 Creating a Custom Camera Class

A good camera system can greatly enhance the player's experience. By default, Unreal Engine uses a simple camera component, but you may want to create a custom camera system to achieve specific effects or gameplay mechanics.

1. **Creating a Camera Manager Class**: Create a new C++ class derived from APlayerCameraManager. Name it *CustomCameraManager*.
2. **Defining Camera Properties**: In the header file, declare variables for zoom levels, camera shake, and camera transitions.
3. **Implementing Dynamic Camera Transitions**: In the source file, write functions to switch between different camera states:

```cpp
Copy code
void ACustomCameraManager::TransitionToZoomedView()
{
    // Logic to smoothly transition the camera to a zoomed-in view
}

void ACustomCameraManager::TransitionToThirdPersonView()
{
    // Logic to switch back to the default third-person view
}
```

### 3.2 Adding Camera Effects with Post-Processing

1. **Setting Up Post-Processing Volumes**: Add a Post-Processing Volume to your level and enable effects such as bloom, depth of field, and motion blur.
2. **Controlling Post-Processing with C++**: In your Camera Manager class, adjust post-processing settings dynamically based on gameplay

events:

```cpp
Copy code
void ACustomCameraManager::ApplyDamageEffect()
{
    // Increase vignette intensity or desaturate the screen when
    the player takes damage
}
```

# Chapter 5: Implementing User Interfaces and HUD Elements

I n today's gaming landscape, user interfaces (UIs) and heads-up displays (HUDs) are crucial components that enhance player experience by providing essential information and controls. Unreal Engine offers robust tools to create dynamic UIs and HUDs that can be easily integrated with gameplay mechanics. In this chapter, we will explore how to implement user interfaces and HUD elements in Unreal Engine using both Blueprints and C++.

We will cover various topics including creating main menus, health and inventory systems, using UMG (Unreal Motion Graphics), binding UI elements to C++ variables, and ensuring that the UI responds to player interactions. By the end of this chapter, you will have a solid understanding of how to design, implement, and optimize UIs in Unreal Engine, enabling you to create intuitive and engaging gameplay experiences.

*Section 1: Introduction to Unreal Motion Graphics (UMG)*

### 1.1 What is UMG?

Unreal Motion Graphics (UMG) is Unreal Engine's built-in tool for creating user interfaces. UMG allows developers to design UI elements using a visual scripting interface, making it accessible for both programmers and designers.

With UMG, you can create menus, HUDs, buttons, sliders, text boxes, and much more, all while leveraging the power of Blueprints and C++.

**1.2 Key Features of UMG**

- **Widgets**: UMG provides a variety of widgets such as buttons, text blocks, images, and progress bars, which can be combined to create complex interfaces.
- **Blueprint Integration**: UMG is tightly integrated with Blueprints, allowing for event-driven interactions and dynamic updates to UI elements.
- **Animations**: UMG supports animations, enabling you to create smooth transitions and effects for your UI.
- **Responsive Design**: UMG allows you to design interfaces that can adapt to different screen sizes and resolutions, ensuring a consistent experience across devices.

## Section 2: Creating a Basic User Interface with UMG

### 2.1 Setting Up the UI Project

To get started with UMG, let's create a simple UI for your game that includes a main menu and a HUD.

1. **Open Your Project**: Make sure you have your Unreal project open.
2. **Creating a New UI Widget**: In the Content Browser, right-click and select *User Interface > Widget Blueprint*. Name it *MainMenuWidget*.
3. **Designing the Main Menu**: Open the *MainMenuWidget* and use the *Designer* tab to layout your menu. Add a *Text Block* for the title and a couple of *Buttons* for starting the game and quitting. Adjust their properties in the Details Panel.

### 2.2 Adding Functionality to the Main Menu

1. **Binding Button Click Events**: Select the start button and navigate to

the *Graph* tab. Right-click in the event graph and add an *OnClicked* event for the button.

2. **Implementing the Start Game Logic**: In the button's click event, add logic to open the main game level. Use the *Open Level* node and specify the name of your game's main level.

```cpp
Copy code
UFUNCTION(BlueprintCallable, Category = "Menu")
void StartGame()
{
    UGameplayStatics::OpenLevel(this, FName(TEXT("MainLevel")));
}
```

1. **Implementing Quit Logic**: For the quit button, use the *Quit Game* node to exit the game when clicked.

### 2.3 Creating a HUD Element

Next, we will create a HUD element that displays the player's health and score.

1. **Creating a HUD Widget**: In the Content Browser, create a new Widget Blueprint and name it *HUDWidget*.
2. **Designing the HUD**: Open *HUDWidget* and add *Text Blocks* for displaying health and score. Use the Details Panel to set their initial text values.

### 2.4 Binding HUD Elements to C++ Variables

To make your HUD dynamic, you need to bind the health and score text to C++ variables.

1. **Creating Variables in C++**: In your player character class (e.g.,

MyCharacter), declare variables for health and score:

```cpp
Copy code
UPROPERTY(BlueprintReadOnly, Category = "Player Stats")
float PlayerHealth;

UPROPERTY(BlueprintReadOnly, Category = "Player Stats")
int32 PlayerScore;
```

1. **Updating the HUD**: Create functions to update the HUD from C++. You can call these functions when the player takes damage or collects items.

```cpp
Copy code
void AMyCharacter::TakeDamage(float DamageAmount)
{
    PlayerHealth -= DamageAmount;
    // Update the HUD here
}

void AMyCharacter::AddScore(int32 Points)
{
    PlayerScore += Points;
    // Update the HUD here
}
```

1. **Binding to the Widget**: In the HUDWidget, use the *Bind* feature to connect the text blocks to the C++ variables. This allows the text blocks to update automatically when the variables change.

## Section 3: Implementing Advanced HUD Features

### 3.1 Adding a Health Bar

A health bar is a common HUD feature that visually represents the player's health.

1. **Creating a Health Bar**: In your *HUDWidget*, add a *Progress Bar* to visually display health. Position it below the score text.
2. **Binding the Progress Bar**: Bind the percentage of the progress bar to the player's health:

```cpp
Copy code
float HealthPercentage = PlayerHealth / MaxHealth; // Calculate
percentage
```

1. **Updating the Progress Bar**: Whenever the health changes, update the progress bar accordingly.

### 3.2 Implementing Inventory UI

Creating an inventory system adds depth to your gameplay. Let's design a simple inventory UI.

1. **Creating an Inventory Widget**: Create a new Widget Blueprint named *InventoryWidget*.
2. **Designing the Inventory**: Add a *Vertical Box* to hold inventory items. Each item can be represented by a *Button* or an *Image*.
3. **Binding Inventory Data**: In your character class, create a function to populate the inventory widget with items collected by the player.

```cpp
Copy code
void AMyCharacter::UpdateInventoryUI()
{
    // Logic to update inventory items in the InventoryWidget
}
```

### 3.3 Animating UI Elements

Animations can enhance the visual appeal of your UI, making it feel more interactive.

1. **Creating UI Animations**: In UMG, select your widget and navigate to the *Animations* tab. Create a new animation that changes the opacity or position of elements.
2. **Triggering Animations**: Use Blueprint logic to trigger animations based on events (e.g., opening the inventory or taking damage).

## Section 4: User Input and Interaction Handling

### 4.1 Setting Up Input Bindings

User input is a critical aspect of gameplay. Unreal Engine allows you to set up input bindings for actions and axes.

1. **Creating Input Bindings**: Go to *Edit > Project Settings > Input* to define new input actions and axes. For example, create an action binding for "Jump" and axis bindings for "Move Forward" and "Turn".
2. **Binding Actions in C++**: In your character class, bind input actions in the SetupPlayerInputComponent function:

```cpp
Copy code
void AMyCharacter::SetupPlayerInputComponent(UInputComponent*
PlayerInputComponent)
```

```
{
    PlayerInputComponent->BindAction("Jump", IE_Pressed, this,
    &ACharacter::Jump);
    PlayerInputComponent->BindAxis("MoveForward", this,
    &AMyCharacter::MoveForward);
}
```

## 4.2 Handling UI Interaction

Implementing user input for UI interactions is crucial for enhancing user experience.

1. **Handling Button Clicks**: In your UMG widget, add click events to buttons (e.g., for starting the game or quitting). Bind these events to functions that will execute when the buttons are clicked.
2. **Mouse Input for UI**: Ensure that your player controller captures mouse input when the UI is open. You can do this by setting the input mode to UI only when the main menu or inventory is displayed.

```cpp
Copy code
void AMyPlayerController::ShowMainMenu()
{
    FInputModeUIOnly InputMode;
    InputMode.SetWidgetToFocus(MainMenuWidget->TakeWidget());
    SetInputMode(InputMode);
    bShowMouseCursor = true;
}
```

## 4.3 Implementing Contextual Actions

For more complex interactions, you may want to implement contextual actions based on the player's proximity to objects.

1. **Using Trace to Detect Objects**: Use line traces to check if the player is near an interactable object. When an object is detected, display contextual prompts (e.g., "Press E to pick up").

2. **Handling Contextual Input**: Bind the context action (e.g., picking up an item) to an input key (like E) and execute the action if the player is near the object.

## Section 5: Optimizing and Finalizing the UI

### 5.1 Performance Considerations

When creating UIs, performance is key to maintaining a smooth gameplay experience.

1. **Limit Draw Calls**: Optimize your UI by minimizing the number of draw calls. Combine textures where possible and use materials efficiently.
2. **Reduce Widget Complexity**: Keep your widgets as lightweight as possible. Use simple designs and avoid excessive animations that could affect performance.

### 5.2 Final Testing and Quality Assurance

Testing your UI is crucial to ensure that it functions as intended.

1. **Playtesting**: Conduct thorough playtests to ensure that the UI is intuitive and responsive. Gather feedback on usability and adjust elements based on player input.
2. **Debugging**: Utilize Unreal Engine's debugging tools to monitor UI performance and troubleshoot any issues that arise.

## Conclusion of Chapter 5

Congratulations on completing Chapter 5! You have learned how to implement user interfaces and HUD elements in Unreal Engine using UMG and C++. From creating basic menus to developing dynamic HUDs and contextual interactions, you now possess the skills needed to enhance player engagement through effective UI design.

In the next chapter, we will explore how to implement audio systems and sound design, further enriching the player experience. Your journey through the world of Unreal Engine and C++ is progressing well, and you are well on your way to mastering game development.

# Chapter 6: Implementing Audio Systems and Sound Design

Audio plays a crucial role in creating immersive gaming experiences. It enhances gameplay by providing feedback, setting the atmosphere, and building emotional connections with players. Unreal Engine offers a robust audio system that allows developers to implement various audio functionalities, from simple sound effects to complex audio environments. In this chapter, we will explore how to effectively use Unreal Engine's audio systems, design soundscapes, and implement dynamic audio interactions in your games.

By the end of this chapter, you will have a comprehensive understanding of audio implementation in Unreal Engine, including sound effects, background music, spatial audio, and advanced audio mixing techniques.

*Section 1: Understanding Unreal Engine's Audio Framework*

### 1.1 Overview of Unreal Engine's Audio System

Unreal Engine's audio system is designed to handle various audio formats, integrate sound effects, manage music tracks, and create spatial audio experiences. The audio framework includes several components that work together to deliver rich audio experiences in your game.

**Key Components**:

- **Sound Cues**: These are assets that allow you to create complex audio behaviors by combining multiple sound waves and adding effects.
- **Sound Waves**: These are the raw audio files (like .wav or .ogg) that contain your audio data.
- **Audio Components**: These are used to play sound in the game world, attached to actors or played as ambient sounds.
- **Sound Mixes**: These allow you to control the overall audio settings and parameters, such as volume and pitch, for different audio classes.

### 1.2 Types of Audio Assets in Unreal

Unreal Engine supports various audio formats, allowing you to utilize high-quality sound files in your games. The most common audio assets include:

- **Sound Wave**: This is the basic audio asset type that contains the actual audio data.
- **Sound Cue**: A Sound Cue combines multiple Sound Waves and can apply effects, volume adjustments, and conditional playback logic.
- **Ambient Sound**: This is an actor that plays sound continuously in the environment, ideal for background noises or environmental sounds.

## Section 2: Importing and Managing Audio Assets

### 2.1 Importing Audio Files

To use audio in Unreal Engine, you need to import audio files into your project.

1. **Supported Formats**: Unreal Engine supports several audio formats, including .wav, .mp3, .ogg, and .aiff. The recommended format for optimal performance and quality is .wav.
2. **Importing Process**:

- Open the Content Browser and right-click in the desired folder.
- Select *Import* and navigate to the location of your audio file.

- Click *Open* to import the audio file into your project.

## 2.2 Creating Sound Cues

Sound Cues allow you to create complex audio behaviors. Let's create a simple Sound Cue for a sound effect.

1. **Creating a New Sound Cue**: Right-click in the Content Browser and select *Sound > Sound Cue*. Name it *S_Cue_ButtonClick*.
2. **Editing the Sound Cue**: Double-click the Sound Cue to open the Sound Cue Editor. Here, you can drag and drop your imported Sound Wave into the graph.
3. **Adding Effects**: You can add various nodes to modify the audio, such as *Random* nodes to play different sound variations or *Attenuation* nodes to control how sound behaves in 3D space.

## 2.3 Managing Audio Assets

Organizing your audio assets is crucial for maintaining a clean project structure. Create folders in the Content Browser for different types of audio, such as *Sound Effects, Music,* and *Ambience*. This organization helps you locate assets quickly during development.

## *Section 3: Implementing Sound Effects*

### 3.1 Playing Sound Effects in C++

Sound effects are essential for providing feedback to players. Let's explore how to implement sound effects using C++.

1. **Creating an Audio Component**: In your character or actor class, declare an audio component to play sound effects.

```cpp
Copy code
UPROPERTY(VisibleAnywhere, BlueprintReadOnly, Category = "Audio")
UAudioComponent* AudioComponent;
```

1. **Initializing the Audio Component**: In the constructor of your class, create the audio component and attach it to the root:

```cpp
Copy code
AMyCharacter::AMyCharacter()
{
    AudioComponent =
    CreateDefaultSubobject<UAudioComponent>(TEXT("AudioComponent"));
    AudioComponent->SetupAttachment(RootComponent);
}
```

1. **Playing a Sound Effect**: Create a function to play a sound effect when an event occurs (e.g., when the player jumps or interacts with an object):

```cpp
Copy code
void AMyCharacter::PlayJumpSound()
{
    if (JumpSoundCue)
    {
        AudioComponent->SetSound(JumpSoundCue);
        AudioComponent->Play();
    }
}
```

## 3.2 Using Sound Effects in Blueprints

1. **Creating Blueprint Variables**: In your character Blueprint, create a variable of type *Sound Cue* for each sound effect you want to use (e.g., jump sound, attack sound).
2. **Playing Sounds in Blueprints**: Use the *Play Sound at Location* node to trigger sound effects based on game events. This node allows you to specify the sound cue and the location where the sound should be played.

## Section 4: Implementing Background Music

### 4.1 Setting Up Background Music

Background music sets the tone and atmosphere for your game. Let's implement a music system using Unreal Engine's audio capabilities.

1. **Importing Background Music**: Import your background music track into the Content Browser.
2. **Creating a Music Player**: Create a new Blueprint actor called *Music-Player* that will handle playing background music.
3. **Adding an Audio Component**: In the MusicPlayer Blueprint, add an Audio Component and set its Sound property to the imported music track.
4. **2 Playing and Controlling Background Music**
5. **Playing Music on Level Start**: In the Event Graph of the MusicPlayer Blueprint, use the *Begin Play* event to start playing the background music.

```blueprint
Copy code
Event BeginPlay→
 Play
```

1. **Controlling Music Volume**: Create a variable to control the volume of the music. You can adjust this variable in the audio component settings

or dynamically based on game events (e.g., when the player enters a quiet area).

### 4.3 Implementing Music Transitions

To create a dynamic audio experience, consider implementing music transitions based on gameplay events. For example, you might want to change the background music when the player enters a combat scenario.

1. **Creating Multiple Music Tracks**: Import different music tracks for different game states (e.g., exploration, combat).
2. **Transition Logic**: In the MusicPlayer Blueprint, use conditions to check the game state. When the player enters combat, stop the current track and play the combat music track instead.

```
blueprint
Copy code
If (Player is in Combat)→
 Stop Current Track→
 Play Combat Music
```

## Section 5: Implementing Spatial Audio and 3D Sound

### 5.1 Understanding Spatial Audio

Spatial audio enhances the immersive experience by simulating how sound behaves in a three-dimensional space. This feature allows players to perceive the direction and distance of sounds, creating a more realistic environment.

### 5.2 Setting Up Spatial Audio

1. **Attenuation Settings**: When creating Sound Cues, you can specify attenuation settings that define how sound decreases in volume over distance. In the Sound Cue Editor, select the Sound Wave and adjust the *Attenuation* settings.

2. **Using Audio Components**: When playing sounds in the game world, attach the audio component to an actor to ensure it plays spatially.

```cpp
Copy code
void AMyActor::PlaySpatialSound()
{
    if (SpatialSoundCue)
    {
        UGameplayStatics::PlaySoundAtLocation(this,
        SpatialSoundCue, GetActorLocation());
    }
}
```

1. **Testing 3D Sound**: Playtest your game to ensure that sounds are coming from the correct locations and attenuating as expected.

## Section 6: Advanced Audio Mixing Techniques

### 6.1 Using Sound Mixes for Audio Control

Sound Mixes allow you to create groups of audio settings that can be adjusted dynamically during gameplay. For example, you can lower the background music when the player is speaking or increase the sound effects volume when the player enters a combat scenario.

1. **Creating a Sound Mix**: In the Content Browser, right-click and select *Sound > Sound Mix*. Name it *GameSoundMix*.
2. **Adding Sound Classes**: Define Sound Classes within the Sound Mix for different audio categories (e.g., UI, Music, Effects). This allows you to control volumes independently.
3. **Adjusting Sound Class Properties**: Set the volume and pitch for each Sound Class in the Sound Mix settings.

## 6.2 Implementing Dynamic Audio Control

1. **Using Audio Volume**: In your game, create events to adjust audio levels dynamically. For instance, when a player enters a dialogue, reduce the volume of the background music:

```cpp
Copy code
UGameplayStatics::AdjustSoundMixVolume(GameSoundMix, 0.5f); //
Reduce to half
```

1. **Restoring Audio Levels**: When the dialogue ends, restore the original audio levels to ensure a seamless experience.

## Section 7: Final Testing and Quality Assurance

### 7.1 Playtesting Audio Implementation

Testing your audio system is crucial to ensure that all sounds function correctly and enhance the gameplay experience.

1. **Conduct Playtests**: Play through your game, paying close attention to how audio interacts with gameplay. Make sure sound effects play at the correct times, music transitions are smooth, and spatial audio works as intended.
2. **Gather Feedback**: Obtain feedback from playtesters regarding the audio experience. Make adjustments based on their input to improve the overall quality of the audio.

### 7.2 Debugging Audio Issues

1. **Using the Audio Debugger**: Unreal Engine includes an audio debugging tool that allows you to monitor active sounds and troubleshoot

any issues. Use this tool to track down problems with sound playback, volume, and attenuation.

2. **Logging Audio Events**: Implement logging in your audio functions to track when sounds are played or when transitions occur. This will help identify any potential issues.

## Conclusion of Chapter 6

Congratulations on completing Chapter 6! You have gained a comprehensive understanding of implementing audio systems and sound design in Unreal Engine using both Blueprints and C++. From setting up sound effects and background music to creating immersive spatial audio experiences, you now have the tools to enhance your game's atmosphere and player engagement through effective audio design.

In the next chapter, we will delve into implementing gameplay systems and mechanics that leverage the audio features you've learned, further enriching the player experience. Your journey through Unreal Engine and C++ is progressing well, and you are well on your way to mastering game development.

This chapter provides a detailed guide to implementing audio systems and sound design in Unreal Engine using C++. It covers the fundamentals of Unreal's audio framework, the process of importing and managing audio assets, creating sound effects, background music, spatial audio, and advanced audio mixing techniques, equipping readers with the skills necessary to create immersive audio experiences in their games.

# Chapter 7: Implementing Game Mechanics and Systems

I n the world of game development, the core mechanics and systems define the gameplay experience. These elements not only engage players but also create the framework through which they interact with your game. Unreal Engine, combined with C++, provides the tools necessary to build complex and engaging game mechanics. In this chapter, we will explore various gameplay systems, including inventory management, quest systems, saving/loading mechanics, and combat systems.

By the end of this chapter, you will have a solid understanding of how to implement these systems effectively using C++ and Unreal Engine's capabilities.

*Section 1: Creating an Inventory System*

### 1.1 Understanding Inventory Mechanics

An inventory system allows players to collect, manage, and utilize items within the game. It can be simple or complex, depending on the game's requirements. Key considerations for an inventory system include:

- **Item Types**: Define various item categories (weapons, consumables, quest items).

- **Item Storage**: Determine how many items can be stored and how they are organized.
- **Usage**: Implement functionality for players to use items, equip weapons, or consume potions.

## 1.2 Designing the Inventory System

1. **Creating Item Classes**: Start by creating a base item class in C++. This class can serve as the parent for all items in the game.

```cpp
Copy code
UCLASS(Blueprintable)
class AItem : public AActor
{
    GENERATED_BODY()

public:
    UPROPERTY(EditAnywhere, BlueprintReadWrite, Category = "Item")
    FString ItemName;

    UPROPERTY(EditAnywhere, BlueprintReadWrite, Category = "Item")
    UTexture2D* ItemIcon;

    UFUNCTION(BlueprintCallable, Category = "Item")
    virtual void Use();
};
```

1. **Deriving Specific Item Types**: Create derived classes for specific item types such as weapons and consumables. Override the Use function to implement unique behavior.

```cpp
Copy code
UCLASS()
class AWeapon : public AItem
{
    GENERATED_BODY()

public:
    UPROPERTY(EditAnywhere, BlueprintReadWrite, Category =
    "Weapon")
    int32 Damage;

    void Use() override;
};
```

1. **Implementing the Inventory Class**: Create a new C++ class for managing the inventory.

```cpp
Copy code
UCLASS()
class AInventory : public UObject
{
    GENERATED_BODY()

private:
    TArray<AItem*> Items;

public:
    void AddItem(AItem* NewItem);
    void RemoveItem(AItem* ItemToRemove);
    TArray<AItem*> GetItems() const;
};
```

## 1.3 Integrating the Inventory System with UI

1. **Creating Inventory UI**: Use UMG to create a simple inventory interface. Include a grid or list to display collected items.
2. **Binding UI to Inventory Data**: In your Inventory class, create a function to populate the UI with the current items. Use Blueprints to bind this data to your inventory widget.

```cpp
cpp
Copy code
void AInventory::UpdateInventoryUI()
{
    // Logic to update the UI elements with current inventory items
}
```

1. **Adding Interactivity**: Implement functionality in your inventory UI to allow players to use or drop items. Use event bindings to trigger these actions.

### 1.4 Testing the Inventory System

1. **Playtesting**: Thoroughly test your inventory system to ensure that items can be collected, used, and removed correctly.
2. **Debugging**: Use debugging tools to track inventory changes and ensure that UI updates reflect the current inventory state.

## Section 2: Implementing a Quest System

### 2.1 Understanding Quest Mechanics

A quest system allows players to engage in tasks or missions, driving the narrative and gameplay. Key components of a quest system include:

- **Quest Types**: Define main quests, side quests, and repeatable quests.
- **Objectives**: Specify the objectives required to complete each quest.

- **Progress Tracking**: Track the player's progress and update quest states dynamically.

## 2.2 Designing the Quest System

1. **Creating a Quest Class**: Start by creating a base quest class in C++. This class can contain properties for quest name, description, objectives, and completion status.

```cpp
Copy code
UCLASS(Blueprintable)
class AQuest : public UObject
{
    GENERATED_BODY()

public:
    UPROPERTY(EditAnywhere, BlueprintReadWrite, Category = "Quest")
    FString QuestName;

    UPROPERTY(EditAnywhere, BlueprintReadWrite, Category = "Quest")
    FString QuestDescription;

    UPROPERTY(EditAnywhere, BlueprintReadWrite, Category = "Quest")
    bool bIsCompleted;

    virtual void CompleteQuest();
};
```

1. **Deriving Specific Quests**: Create derived classes for specific quests, such as collection quests or kill quests. Override the CompleteQuest function to implement unique completion logic.

```cpp
Copy code
UCLASS()
class ACollectionQuest : public AQuest
{
    GENERATED_BODY()

public:
    UPROPERTY(EditAnywhere, BlueprintReadWrite, Category = "Quest")
    int32 RequiredItems;

    void CompleteQuest() override;
};
```

1. **Implementing the Quest Manager**: Create a Quest Manager class to handle active quests and their progression.

```cpp
Copy code
UCLASS()
class AQuestManager : public UObject
{
    GENERATED_BODY()

private:
    TArray<AQuest*> ActiveQuests;

public:
    void AddQuest(AQuest* NewQuest);
    void UpdateQuestProgress(AQuest* Quest, int32 Progress);
};
```

## 2.3 Integrating the Quest System with UI

1. **Creating Quest UI**: Use UMG to design a quest log interface where players can view active quests and their objectives.

2. **Binding UI to Quest Data**: In your Quest Manager class, create a function to populate the quest log with current quests. Bind this data to your quest log widget.

```cpp
Copy code
void AQuestManager::UpdateQuestLogUI()
{
    // Logic to update the UI elements with current quests
}
```

1. **Adding Interactivity**: Implement functionality in your quest UI to allow players to track their quests, view objectives, and mark quests as complete.

### 2.4 Testing the Quest System

1. **Playtesting**: Test the quest system to ensure quests can be added, tracked, and completed correctly.
2. **Debugging**: Use debugging tools to monitor quest progression and ensure that the UI updates appropriately.

## Section 3: Implementing Saving and Loading Mechanics

### 3.1 Understanding Save Game Systems

A save game system allows players to save their progress and return to it later. Key considerations for a save game system include:

- **Data Storage**: Determine what data to save (player progress, inventory, quests).
- **Serialization**: Implement functionality to convert game data into a format suitable for storage (e.g., JSON or binary).

## 3.2 Designing the Save Game System

1. **Creating a Save Game Class**: Create a new C++ class derived from USaveGame that will store player data.

```cpp
Copy code
UCLASS()
class USaveGameData : public USaveGame
{
    GENERATED_BODY()

public:
    UPROPERTY(VisibleAnywhere, BlueprintReadWrite)
    float PlayerHealth;

    UPROPERTY(VisibleAnywhere, BlueprintReadWrite)
    TArray<FString> InventoryItems;

    UPROPERTY(VisibleAnywhere, BlueprintReadWrite)
    TArray<FString> ActiveQuests;
};
```

1. **Implementing Save Logic**: Create functions in your character class to save and load game data.

```cpp
Copy code
void AMyCharacter::SaveGame()
{
    USaveGameData* SaveGameInstance
= Cast<USaveGameData>(UGameplayStatics:
:CreateSaveGameObject
```

```
(USaveGameData::StaticClass()));
    SaveGameInstance->PlayerHealth = PlayerHealth;
    SaveGameInstance->InventoryItems
= Inventory->GetItems();
// Assuming you have a method to get inventory items

    UGameplayStatics::
SaveGameToSlot(SaveGameInstance,
TEXT("PlayerSave"), 0);
}

void AMyCharacter::LoadGame()
{
    USaveGameData* LoadGameInstance =
 Cast<USaveGameData>(UGameplayStatics::
LoadGameFromSlot
(TEXT("PlayerSave"), 0));
    if (LoadGameInstance)
    {
        PlayerHealth = LoadGameInstance->PlayerHealth;
        Inventory->SetItems
(LoadGameInstance->InventoryItems);
// Assuming you have a method to set inventory items
    }
}
```

## 3.3 Integrating Save/Load with UI

1. **Creating Save/Load UI**: Use UMG to create a simple UI for saving and loading games.

2. **Binding UI to Save/Load Functions**: Implement buttons in the UI that call the SaveGame and LoadGame functions when clicked.

3. **4 Testing the Save/Load System**

4. **Playtesting**: Thoroughly test the save and load functionalities to ensure data is correctly saved and retrieved.

5. **Debugging**: Use logs to monitor the saving and loading processes, checking for any data inconsistencies or errors.

## Section 4: Implementing Combat Systems

### 4.1 Understanding Combat Mechanics

Combat systems are central to many games, providing players with a way to engage with enemies and challenges. Key considerations for a combat system include:

- **Character Abilities**: Define how players can attack, defend, and use abilities.
- **Enemy AI**: Implement AI behavior for enemies to create challenging combat scenarios.
- **Health and Damage Systems**: Track player and enemy health and implement damage calculations.

### 4.2 Designing the Combat System

1. **Creating an Attack Mechanic**: In your character class, implement a function to handle attacks.

```cpp
Copy code
void AMyCharacter::Attack()
{
    // Logic to perform an attack (e.g., playing an animation,
    dealing damage)
}
```

1. **Implementing Hit Detection**: Use collision detection or ray tracing to determine if an attack hits an enemy.

```cpp
Copy code
void AMyCharacter::PerformAttack()
{
    FHitResult Hit;
    FVector Start = GetActorLocation();
    FVector End = Start + GetActorForwardVector()
* AttackRange;

    FCollisionQueryParams CollisionParams;
    if (GetWorld()->LineTraceSingleByChannel
(Hit, Start, End, ECC_GameTraceChannel2,
 CollisionParams))
    {
        AEnemy* HitEnemy = Cast
<AEnemy>(Hit.GetActor());
        if (HitEnemy)
        {
            HitEnemy->TakeDamage(AttackDamage);
        }
    }
}
```

1. **Implementing Damage System**: Create a function in your enemy class to handle damage:

```cpp
Copy code
void AEnemy::TakeDamage(float DamageAmount)
{
    Health -= DamageAmount;
    if (Health <= 0)
    {
        // Handle enemy death
    }
}
```

### 4.3 Integrating Enemy AI in Combat

1. **Creating an Enemy Class**: Create a new C++ class for enemies that includes AI behavior and combat logic.
2. **Implementing AI Combat Logic**: Use Behavior Trees and Blackboards to define enemy combat behavior, such as attacking when the player is in range or retreating when low on health.

### 4.4 Adding Animations for Combat

1. **Setting Up Combat Animations**: Create animation states for various combat actions, including idle, attack, and death.
2. **Triggering Animations in C++**: Use animation montages to trigger combat animations when attacks are performed.

```cpp
Copy code
void AMyCharacter::PlayAttackAnimation()
{
    if (AttackAnimationMontage)
    {
        PlayAnimMontage(AttackAnimationMontage);
    }
}
```

### 4.5 Testing the Combat System

1. **Playtesting**: Test the combat mechanics to ensure attacks register correctly and enemies respond appropriately.
2. **Balancing**: Adjust damage values, attack speeds, and enemy AI behavior to create a balanced combat experience.

## *Conclusion of Chapter 7*

Congratulations on completing Chapter 7! You have learned how to implement various game mechanics and systems using C++ in Unreal Engine. From creating an inventory system and quest mechanics to developing saving/loading functionalities and combat systems, you now possess the knowledge to build complex gameplay experiences that engage players.

In the next chapter, we will explore how to integrate multiplayer functionality into your game, allowing players to interact and compete in shared environments. Your journey through Unreal Engine and C++ is progressing well, and you are well on your way to mastering game development.

This chapter provides a thorough exploration of implementing various gameplay mechanics and systems in Unreal Engine using C++. It covers the design and implementation of inventory systems, quest systems, saving/loading mechanics, and combat systems, equipping readers with the skills necessary to create engaging and interactive gameplay experiences.

# Chapter 8: Integrating Multiplayer Functionality

I n the modern gaming landscape, multiplayer functionality is essential for engaging players and creating dynamic experiences. Whether it's cooperative gameplay, competitive modes, or shared world interactions, multiplayer mechanics add depth and excitement to any game. Unreal Engine provides robust tools and frameworks for implementing multiplayer features, allowing developers to create seamless online experiences.

In this chapter, we will explore how to integrate multiplayer functionality into your game using C++. We'll cover the fundamentals of networking in Unreal, implement basic multiplayer features, handle replication for gameplay elements, and discuss advanced topics like matchmaking and server management. By the end of this chapter, you will have the skills necessary to develop a fully functional multiplayer game.

*Section 1: Understanding Networking in Unreal Engine*

### 1.1 Overview of Networking Concepts

Networking in Unreal Engine is built around the client-server model, where a server hosts the game and multiple clients connect to it. Understanding key networking concepts is vital for implementing multiplayer functionality.

**Key Concepts:**

- **Client**: A player's instance of the game that connects to the server.
- **Server**: The authoritative instance that manages game logic, player states, and interactions.
- **Replication**: The process of synchronizing data between the server and clients, ensuring that all players see the same game state.
- **RPC (Remote Procedure Call)**: A method for invoking functions across the network. RPCs allow clients to call server functions and vice versa.

### 1.2 Setting Up a Multiplayer Project

1. **Creating a New Project**: Start by creating a new project in Unreal Engine and ensure you select the *Third Person* template for convenience.
2. **Configuring Project Settings**: Navigate to *Edit > Project Settings > Maps & Modes* and set the *Game Default Map* to a map that will serve as your multiplayer lobby.

### 1.3 Understanding Unreal's Networking Architecture

Unreal Engine abstracts many of the complexities involved in networking through its built-in systems. Key components include:

- **GameMode**: Defines the rules of the game, including how players join and leave.
- **PlayerController**: Manages player input and interaction with the game world.
- **GameState**: Holds game-specific information that needs to be replicated across clients, such as scores and player states.

## Section 2: Implementing Basic Multiplayer Functionality

### 2.1 Setting Up Player Spawning

1. **Custom GameMode Class**: Create a custom GameMode class that will handle player spawning. In your CustomGameMode.h, define the

necessary functions:

```cpp
Copy code
UCLASS()
class ACustomGameMode : public AGameModeBase
{
    GENERATED_BODY()

public:
    virtual void StartPlay() override;
};
```

1. **Implementing Player Spawning**: In CustomGameMode.cpp, override the StartPlay method to spawn players:

```cpp
Copy code
void ACustomGameMode::StartPlay()
{
    Super::StartPlay();

    for (FConstPlayerControllerIterator It =
    GetWorld()->GetPlayerControllerIterator(); It; ++It)
    {
        APlayerController* PlayerController = It->Get();
        if (PlayerController)
        {
            // Spawn player character here
        }
    }
}
```

## 2.2 Handling Player Input and Interaction

1. **Custom PlayerController Class**: Create a custom PlayerController class that manages player input. In CustomPlayerController.h:

```cpp
Copy code
UCLASS()
class ACustomPlayerController : public APlayerController
{
    GENERATED_BODY()

public:
    virtual void SetupInputComponent() override;
};
```

1. **Implementing Input Handling**: In CustomPlayerController.cpp, set up input bindings:

```cpp
Copy code
void ACustomPlayerController::SetupInputComponent()
{
    Super::SetupInputComponent();
    InputComponent->BindAction("Jump", IE_Pressed, this,
    &ACharacter::Jump);
    InputComponent->BindAxis("MoveForward", this,
    &ACustomPlayerController::MoveForward);
}
```

## 2.3 Building a Simple Multiplayer Game Level

1. **Creating the Game Level**: Design a simple level that includes spawn points for players. Use a *Player Start* actor to define where players will spawn when joining the game.
2. **Testing Multiplayer Functionality**: Launch the game in *Play* mode

and test with multiple players. Use the *Standalone* mode or *New Editor Window* to simulate multiple clients.

## Section 3: Implementing Replication and Synchronization

### 3.1 Understanding Replication

Replication is the process of synchronizing variables and functions across the server and clients. Unreal Engine provides built-in support for replication, allowing developers to easily share data between instances.

**Key Replication Concepts**:

- **Replicated Variables**: Variables that are marked for replication will automatically sync their values between the server and clients.
- **Replicated Functions**: Functions can be marked as RPCs to ensure they execute on the server or clients as needed.

### 3.2 Replicating Variables in C++

1. **Marking Variables for Replication**: In your character class, declare variables that need to be replicated using the UPROPERTY macro.

```cpp
Copy code
UPROPERTY(ReplicatedUsing = OnRep_Health)
float Health;

UFUNCTION()
void OnRep_Health();
```

1. **Implementing Replication Logic**: In the character class, implement the GetLifetimeReplicatedProps function to specify which variables to replicate.

```cpp
Copy code
void
AMyCharacter::GetLifetimeReplicatedProps(TArray<FLifetimeProperty>&
OutLifetimeProps) const
{
    Super::GetLifetimeReplicatedProps(OutLifetimeProps);
    DOREPLIFETIME(AMyCharacter, Health);
}
```

## 3.3 Replicating Functions

1. **Creating Remote Procedure Calls**: Implement functions that should be called on the server or clients. Use the UFUNCTION macro to specify if the function is a client or server RPC.

```cpp
Copy code
UFUNCTION(Server, Reliable)
void ServerTakeDamage(float DamageAmount);
```

1. **Implementing the Server Function**: In your character class, define the server function that handles damage:

```cpp
Copy code
void AMyCharacter::ServerTakeDamage_Implementation(float
DamageAmount)
{
    TakeDamage(DamageAmount); // Calls the local function to
    handle damage
```

```
}
```

## 3.4 Handling Client-Server Communication

1. **Using Client RPCs**: Create functions to send information from the server to clients. For example, when a player's health changes, you can notify all clients:

```cpp
Copy code
UFUNCTION(Client, Reliable)
void ClientUpdateHealth(float NewHealth);
```

1. **Implementing Client Function**: Define the client function to update the health UI on each client:

```cpp
Copy code
void AMyCharacter::ClientUpdateHealth_Implementation(float
NewHealth)
{
    Health = NewHealth;
    // Update UI or perform any necessary actions
}
```

## Section 4: Advanced Multiplayer Features

### 4.1 Implementing Matchmaking and Server Browsing

1. **Understanding Online Subsystems**: Unreal Engine provides online subsystems to manage multiplayer connections. Depending on the

platform (Steam, Xbox, etc.), the online subsystem varies.

2. **Setting Up Online Subsystem**: In your project settings, enable the relevant online subsystem for your target platform.

3. **Implementing Matchmaking**: Use the Online Subsystem API to implement matchmaking features. Create functions to host or join sessions based on player input.

4. **2 Server Management**

5. **Creating Dedicated Servers**: Create dedicated server builds to manage online sessions. Set up command-line arguments to launch your game as a server.

6. **Server Administration**: Implement administrative functions for managing sessions, including kicking players or changing game settings.

## 4.3 Handling Player Connections and Disconnections

1. **Managing Player Connections**: In your GameMode, override the PostLogin and Logout functions to manage player connections.

```cpp
Copy code
void ACustomGameMode::PostLogin(APlayerController* NewPlayer)
{
    Super::PostLogin(NewPlayer);
    // Logic to handle new player connections
}

void ACustomGameMode::Logout(AController* Exiting)
{
    Super::Logout(Exiting);
    // Logic to clean up when a player leaves
}
```

1. **Handling Player States**: Maintain player state information, such as health and inventory, across connections and disconnections.

## Section 5: Testing and Debugging Multiplayer Games

### 5.1 Playtesting Multiplayer Functionality

1. **Testing with Multiple Clients**: Use the *Standalone* mode to simulate multiple players. Launch the game and test all multiplayer features, including spawning, input handling, and interaction.
2. **Network Simulation**: Unreal Engine allows you to simulate network conditions (like latency and packet loss) during playtesting to identify potential issues.

### 5.2 Debugging Multiplayer Issues

1. **Using the Network Profiler**: Unreal Engine includes a Network Profiler tool to monitor network performance and identify bottlenecks or replication issues.
2. **Logging and Debugging**: Implement logging in your multiplayer functions to track player connections, RPC calls, and other critical events. Use logs to troubleshoot any issues that arise during testing.

## Conclusion of Chapter 8

Congratulations on completing Chapter 8! You have gained a comprehensive understanding of how to integrate multiplayer functionality into your Unreal Engine projects using C++. From setting up player spawning and handling input to implementing replication and advanced multiplayer features, you now have the tools to create engaging online experiences.

In the next chapter, we will explore how to optimize your game for performance, ensuring that your multiplayer experience is smooth and enjoyable for all players. Your journey through Unreal Engine and C++ is progressing well, and you are well on your way to mastering game development.

This chapter provides a thorough exploration of integrating multiplayer functionality into Unreal Engine using C++. It covers the fundamentals of networking, player input handling, replication, and advanced features like matchmaking and server management, equipping readers with the skills necessary to develop engaging multiplayer experiences.

# Chapter 9: Optimizing Game Performance

I n the competitive landscape of game development, optimizing your game's performance is crucial to providing players with a smooth and engaging experience. Unreal Engine offers numerous tools and techniques to enhance performance, reduce load times, and ensure that your game runs efficiently on a variety of hardware. In this chapter, we will explore strategies for optimizing your game in Unreal Engine, focusing on graphics, gameplay mechanics, memory management, and network performance.

By the end of this chapter, you will have a comprehensive understanding of how to implement optimization techniques, conduct performance profiling, and address common performance issues in your Unreal Engine projects.

*Section 1: Understanding Performance Metrics*

### 1.1 Key Performance Metrics

Before diving into optimization techniques, it's essential to understand the key performance metrics that developers should monitor:

- **Frame Rate (FPS)**: The number of frames rendered per second. A higher FPS generally indicates a smoother gameplay experience.
- **CPU and GPU Usage**: The percentage of CPU and GPU resources used

during gameplay. High usage can lead to performance bottlenecks.

- **Memory Usage**: The amount of RAM consumed by the game. Excessive memory usage can result in crashes or slowdowns.
- **Load Times**: The time it takes to load levels and assets. Reducing load times improves player experience.

### 1.2 Tools for Measuring Performance

Unreal Engine provides several built-in tools to measure and profile game performance:

- **Stat Commands**: Use console commands such as stat fps, stat cpu, and stat memory to display real-time performance metrics.
- **Unreal Insights**: A powerful profiling tool that helps you analyze performance data, including frame timing, memory allocation, and CPU/GPU usage.
- **Profile GPU**: This command helps you understand GPU performance, including shader compilation times and draw calls.

## Section 2: Graphics Optimization Techniques

### 2.1 Level of Detail (LOD)

Level of Detail (LOD) is a technique used to reduce the complexity of 3D models based on their distance from the camera. By displaying simpler models for objects that are further away, you can significantly reduce the rendering load.

1. **Creating LODs for Static Meshes**: In the static mesh editor, create multiple versions of your mesh with varying levels of detail. Set up LOD thresholds to automatically switch between these models based on camera distance.
2. **2 Culling Techniques**

Culling is the process of not rendering objects that are not visible to the camera, reducing the workload on the GPU.

1. **Frustum Culling**: Unreal Engine automatically culls objects outside the camera's view. However, you can further optimize by using bounding volumes to define visibility.
2. **Occlusion Culling**: This technique prevents rendering objects blocked by other objects. Implement occlusion volumes in your levels to enhance performance.

## 2.3 Texture Optimization

Textures are one of the most memory-intensive components of a game. Optimizing textures can lead to significant performance gains.

1. **Texture Size Reduction**: Use the appropriate texture resolution for your assets. Consider using lower resolutions for distant objects and high resolutions for close-up details.
2. **Texture Compression**: Use texture compression settings in Unreal Engine to reduce memory usage without significantly affecting quality.

## 2.4 Efficient Material Usage

Materials can also impact performance, especially when using complex shaders.

1. **Material Instances**: Instead of creating unique materials for every variation, use material instances to create variations of a base material, reducing draw calls.
2. **Minimize Texture Sample Nodes**: Each texture sample in a material adds processing overhead. Minimize the number of samples used in your materials, especially for objects rendered frequently.

## Section 3: Gameplay Optimization Techniques

### 3.1 Blueprint Optimization
While Blueprints offer an easy way to implement gameplay mechanics, poorly designed Blueprints can lead to performance issues.

1. **Avoiding Tick Events**: The Tick event can be costly if used extensively. Use event-driven programming wherever possible, and avoid unnecessary Tick calls.
2. **Using Functions Over Macros**: Functions have a lower performance impact compared to macros, especially in large Blueprints. Use functions for complex logic.
3. **2 Efficient Actor Management**

Managing the lifecycle of actors in your game is critical for performance.

1. **Pooling Actors**: Instead of destroying and creating actors repeatedly, implement an object pool to reuse actors. This technique is particularly useful for projectile or enemy spawning.
2. **Batching Actor Updates**: Group similar actors and update them together to reduce overhead. For example, update all enemies' AI states in a single function call rather than individually.
3. **3 Physics Optimization**

Physics calculations can be expensive, especially when many objects interact simultaneously.

1. **Adjusting Physics Properties**: Use simpler collision shapes (like box or sphere colliders) instead of complex meshes. Reduce the number of physics ticks if not necessary.
2. **Controlling Physics Simulations**: Use physics settings to control how objects react to forces. Consider using kinematic physics for objects that do not require full physics simulation.

## Section 4: Memory Management

### 4.1 Understanding Memory Usage

Memory management is essential for maintaining performance and stability in your game. Monitor memory usage to prevent leaks and ensure optimal performance.

1. **Garbage Collection**: Unreal Engine uses a garbage collection system to manage memory. Understand how garbage collection works and how to manage object lifetimes to minimize performance hits.
2. **Profiling Memory**: Use the stat memory command to analyze memory usage in real-time. This tool helps identify areas where memory can be optimized.

### 4.2 Asset Management

Managing game assets effectively can prevent excessive memory consumption.

1. **Asset Streaming**: Use Unreal's streaming features to load and unload assets dynamically based on player proximity or visibility. This technique reduces memory usage by only keeping necessary assets in memory.
2. **Texture Atlases**: Combine multiple textures into a single texture atlas to reduce the number of texture bindings, which can improve performance.

## Section 5: Network Performance Optimization

### 5.1 Understanding Network Latency and Bandwidth

In multiplayer games, network latency and bandwidth can significantly impact performance and gameplay experience. Understanding these factors is essential for optimizing network performance.

1. **Latency**: The delay between sending and receiving data over the network. High latency can lead to laggy gameplay experiences.

2. **Bandwidth**: The amount of data that can be transmitted over the network in a given time. Managing bandwidth is crucial for ensuring that data is sent and received efficiently.

## 5.2 Reducing Network Traffic

1. **Optimizing Replication**: Only replicate necessary variables to minimize the amount of data sent over the network. Use conditions to determine when replication is needed.
2. **Using Efficient Data Formats**: When sending data over the network, use efficient data formats (e.g., bitwise flags) to reduce the amount of data transmitted.

## 5.3 Client-Side Prediction

Implement client-side prediction to improve the responsiveness of player actions.

1. **Local Prediction**: Allow clients to predict the outcome of their actions (e.g., movement) before receiving confirmation from the server. This technique reduces perceived latency and improves gameplay feel.
2. **Reconciliation**: Handle discrepancies between server and client states by reconciling data when server updates arrive.

## Section 6: Profiling and Performance Testing

### 6.1 Performance Profiling

Profiling is a critical step in optimizing your game. Unreal Engine provides several profiling tools to help identify performance bottlenecks.

1. **Using Unreal Insights**: This tool allows you to analyze performance data over time. Record sessions while playing the game to identify areas that need optimization.
2. **Stat Commands**: Utilize stat commands to get real-time performance

data. For example, use stat unit to view frame time, game time, and render time.

## 6.2 Conducting Performance Tests

1. **Testing on Multiple Hardware**: Test your game on various hardware configurations to identify performance issues that may arise on lower-end systems.
2. **Simulating Network Conditions**: Use network simulation tools to test how your game performs under different latency and packet loss scenarios.

## Conclusion of Chapter 9

Congratulations on completing Chapter 9! You have learned essential techniques for optimizing game performance in Unreal Engine using C++. From graphics optimization and gameplay mechanics to memory management and network performance, you now possess the skills to enhance your game's efficiency and responsiveness.

In the next chapter, we will explore the integration of additional features such as user settings, modding support, and how to prepare your game for release. Your journey through Unreal Engine and C++ is progressing well, and you are well on your way to mastering game development.

This chapter provides a thorough exploration of performance optimization techniques in Unreal Engine using C++. It covers key metrics, optimization strategies for graphics and gameplay, memory management, network performance, and profiling methods, equipping readers with the skills necessary to create efficient and engaging gameplay experiences.

4o mini

You said:

write in 7000 words Chapter 10

ChatGPT said:

ChatGPT

Here's a comprehensive draft for *Chapter 10: Preparing Your Game for Release* of *Develop High Quality Video Games with C++ and Unreal Engine*, aimed at approximately 7,000 words.

# Chapter 10: Preparing Your Game for Release

As you approach the final stages of game development, it's essential to prepare your game for release meticulously. This chapter will guide you through the necessary steps to ensure your game is polished, optimized, and ready for players. We will cover topics such as finalizing gameplay features, creating build configurations, implementing user settings, preparing for different platforms, and marketing strategies. By the end of this chapter, you will have a comprehensive understanding of the release process, allowing you to launch your game successfully.

## *Section 1: Finalizing Gameplay Features*

### 1.1 Conducting Thorough Testing

Before releasing your game, thorough testing is essential to ensure a smooth experience for players. This includes playtesting, bug testing, and quality assurance (QA) processes.

1. **Internal Playtesting**: Gather a team of testers who can provide feedback on gameplay mechanics, controls, and overall experience. Ensure that your testers play through the game multiple times to identify any potential issues.
2. **Beta Testing**: Consider conducting a closed or open beta test to gather feedback from external players. This can help identify bugs and gameplay imbalances that internal testers may have missed.
3. **Bug Tracking**: Use a bug tracking system (such as Jira or Trello) to document and prioritize bugs. Ensure that each bug is assigned to a

team member for resolution.

## 1.2 Polishing Game Features

After testing, focus on polishing your game's features based on the feedback received.

1. **Adjusting Game Balance**: Analyze player feedback to identify areas where gameplay balance may need adjustment. This may include tweaking enemy difficulty, adjusting player abilities, or fine-tuning item statistics.
2. **Refining User Experience (UX)**: Ensure that the user interface is intuitive and easy to navigate. Gather feedback on menus, HUD elements, and inventory systems to make necessary adjustments.

## Section 2: Building Configurations

### 2.1 Understanding Build Configurations

Unreal Engine supports multiple build configurations, allowing you to create different versions of your game for testing and release. Common configurations include:

- **Development**: Used for debugging and testing. Includes debugging symbols and other development features.
- **Shipping**: The final version of the game for release. Optimized for performance and lacks debugging information.
- **Test**: A version that combines elements of both development and shipping, used primarily for internal testing.

### 2.2 Creating a Shipping Build

1. **Setting Build Configuration**: In the Unreal Editor, navigate to *File > Package Project* and select your desired platform. Ensure that you choose the *Shipping* configuration.

2. **Configuring Project Settings**: Go to *Edit > Project Settings* and review the settings under the *Packaging* section. Ensure that you have selected appropriate options for your game, including compression and file paths.
3. **Packaging Your Game**: Follow the prompts to package your game. Unreal Engine will create a build for the selected platform, ready for distribution.

**2.3 Testing the Shipping Build**

Once the shipping build is created, thoroughly test it to ensure all gameplay features work as expected without debugging information.

1. **Playtesting the Shipping Build**: Test the build on the target platform to verify performance and stability. Check for any issues that may not have appeared in the development build.
2. **Performance Profiling**: Use profiling tools to analyze performance in the shipping build, ensuring that frame rates and load times meet your standards.

## Section 3: Implementing User Settings

**3.1 Understanding User Preferences**

Implementing user settings allows players to customize their gameplay experience. Key settings may include graphics options, audio levels, control mappings, and accessibility features.

**3.2 Creating a User Settings Menu**

1. **Designing the Settings UI**: Use UMG to create a user settings menu that allows players to adjust various options. Include sliders for volume, dropdowns for graphics settings, and buttons for control mappings.
2. **Binding Settings to Variables**: In your settings menu, bind UI elements to C++ variables that represent user preferences.

```cpp
Copy code
UFUNCTION(BlueprintCallable, Category = "Settings")
void SetVolume(float NewVolume);
```

1. **Saving User Preferences**: Implement functionality to save user preferences using Unreal's Save Game system. Create a Save Game class to
   store these settings.

```cpp
Copy code
void UMyGameInstance::SaveUserSettings()
{
    USaveGameData* SaveGameInstance =
Cast<USaveGameData>(UGameplayStatics:
:CreateSaveGameObject
(USaveGameData::StaticClass()));
    SaveGameInstance->Volume = CurrentVolume;
    SaveGameInstance->GraphicsQuality =
 CurrentGraphicsQuality;

    UGameplayStatics::SaveGameToSlot
(SaveGameInstance,
TEXT("UserSettings"), 0);
}
```

### 3.3 Loading User Preferences

1. **Loading Settings on Start**: When the game starts, load the saved user
   preferences and apply them to the game settings. This ensures that
   players' settings are retained across sessions.

```cpp
Copy code
void UMyGameInstance::LoadUserSettings()
{
    USaveGameData* LoadGameInstance =
 Cast<USaveGameData>
(UGameplayStatics::LoadGameFromSlot
(TEXT("UserSettings"), 0));
    if (LoadGameInstance)
    {
        CurrentVolume = LoadGameInstance->Volume;
        CurrentGraphicsQuality =
 LoadGameInstance->GraphicsQuality;
    }
}
```

# Section 4: Preparing for Different Platforms

### 4.1 Platform-Specific Considerations

When preparing your game for release, consider the specific requirements and guidelines for each platform (PC, consoles, mobile).

1. **Performance Optimization**: Optimize your game for the target platform's hardware specifications. For example, mobile games may require lower resolutions and simplified graphics.
2. **Input Management**: Ensure that your game supports various input methods. For example, console games should support gamepad input, while PC games may require keyboard and mouse controls.

### 4.2 Packaging for Different Platforms

1. **Platform-Specific Packaging**: Use the *Package Project* option in Unreal Engine to create builds for each target platform. Ensure that you configure settings specific to each platform.
2. **Testing on Target Platforms**: Thoroughly test your game on each

target platform to identify and resolve any platform-specific issues.

## Section 5: Marketing Strategies for Your Game

### 5.1 Developing a Marketing Plan

A successful marketing strategy is essential for generating interest in your game. Develop a plan that outlines your target audience, marketing channels, and promotional activities.

1. **Identifying Your Target Audience**: Understand who your game appeals to and tailor your marketing messages accordingly. Consider demographics, interests, and gaming preferences.
2. **Choosing Marketing Channels**: Select the most effective channels for reaching your audience, including social media, gaming forums, and influencer partnerships.

### 5.2 Creating Promotional Material

1. **Trailers and Gameplay Videos**: Produce high-quality trailers that showcase your game's features and gameplay mechanics. These videos can be shared on platforms like YouTube and social media.
2. **Screenshots and Art Assets**: Capture engaging screenshots and create promotional art assets to use in marketing materials. Ensure these images highlight the game's unique aspects.

### 5.3 Engaging with the Community

1. **Building a Community**: Engage with players through social media, forums, and Discord. Create a community around your game to foster loyalty and gather feedback.
2. **Hosting Events**: Consider hosting events such as livestreams, Q&A sessions, or beta tests to generate excitement and involve players in the development process.

## Section 6: Launching Your Game

### 6.1 Preparing for Launch Day

As launch day approaches, ensure that all aspects of your game are ready for public consumption.

1. **Final Checks**: Perform a final round of testing to catch any last-minute issues. Confirm that all marketing materials are in place and that your community is engaged and informed about the launch.
2. **Set Up Distribution Platforms**: Ensure that your game is set up for distribution on platforms such as Steam, Epic Games Store, or console stores. Familiarize yourself with their submission processes and requirements.

### 6.2 Post-Launch Support

1. **Monitoring Player Feedback**: After the game launches, actively monitor player feedback and reviews. Use this information to identify areas for improvement or bugs that need addressing.
2. **Implementing Updates**: Plan for post-launch updates to address bugs, balance gameplay, and add new content based on player feedback. Keep your community informed about upcoming updates and changes.

## Conclusion of Chapter 10

Congratulations on completing Chapter 10! You have gained a comprehensive understanding of how to prepare your game for release using Unreal Engine and C++. From finalizing gameplay features and optimizing performance to implementing user settings and marketing strategies, you now have the skills necessary to launch your game successfully.

In the next chapter, we will explore how to analyze player data and implement game analytics to improve player engagement and retention. Your journey through Unreal Engine and C++ is progressing well, and you are well on your way to mastering game development.

This chapter provides a thorough exploration of preparing your game for release in Unreal Engine using C++. It covers key aspects such as finalizing gameplay features, building configurations, implementing user settings, preparing for different platforms, and marketing strategies, equipping readers with the skills necessary to launch their games successfully.

# Chapter 10: Preparing Your Game for Release

As you approach the final stages of game development, it's essential to prepare your game for release meticulously. This chapter will guide you through the necessary steps to ensure your game is polished, optimized, and ready for players. We will cover topics such as finalizing gameplay features, creating build configurations, implementing user settings, preparing for different platforms, and marketing strategies. By the end of this chapter, you will have a comprehensive understanding of the release process, allowing you to launch your game successfully.

*Section 1: Finalizing Gameplay Features*

### 1.1 Conducting Thorough Testing

Before releasing your game, thorough testing is essential to ensure a smooth experience for players. This includes playtesting, bug testing, and quality assurance (QA) processes.

1. **Internal Playtesting**: Gather a team of testers who can provide feedback on gameplay mechanics, controls, and overall experience. Ensure that your testers play through the game multiple times to identify any potential issues.

2. **Beta Testing**: Consider conducting a closed or open beta test to gather feedback from external players. This can help identify bugs and gameplay imbalances that internal testers may have missed.
3. **Bug Tracking**: Use a bug tracking system (such as Jira or Trello) to document and prioritize bugs. Ensure that each bug is assigned to a team member for resolution.

### 1.2 Polishing Game Features

After testing, focus on polishing your game's features based on the feedback received.

1. **Adjusting Game Balance**: Analyze player feedback to identify areas where gameplay balance may need adjustment. This may include tweaking enemy difficulty, adjusting player abilities, or fine-tuning item statistics.
2. **Refining User Experience (UX)**: Ensure that the user interface is intuitive and easy to navigate. Gather feedback on menus, HUD elements, and inventory systems to make necessary adjustments.

## Section 2: Building Configurations

### 2.1 Understanding Build Configurations

Unreal Engine supports multiple build configurations, allowing you to create different versions of your game for testing and release. Common configurations include:

- **Development**: Used for debugging and testing. Includes debugging symbols and other development features.
- **Shipping**: The final version of the game for release. Optimized for performance and lacks debugging information.
- **Test**: A version that combines elements of both development and shipping, used primarily for internal testing.

## 2.2 Creating a Shipping Build

1. **Setting Build Configuration**: In the Unreal Editor, navigate to *File >
   Package Project* and select your desired platform. Ensure that you choose
   the *Shipping* configuration.
2. **Configuring Project Settings**: Go to *Edit > Project Settings* and review
   the settings under the *Packaging* section. Ensure that you have selected
   appropriate options for your game, including compression and file paths.
3. **Packaging Your Game**: Follow the prompts to package your game.
   Unreal Engine will create a build for the selected platform, ready for
   distribution.

## 2.3 Testing the Shipping Build

Once the shipping build is created, thoroughly test it to ensure all gameplay
features work as expected without debugging information.

1. **Playtesting the Shipping Build**: Test the build on the target platform
   to verify performance and stability. Check for any issues that may not
   have appeared in the development build.
2. **Performance Profiling**: Use profiling tools to analyze performance in
   the shipping build, ensuring that frame rates and load times meet your
   standards.

## Section 3: Implementing User Settings

## 3.1 Understanding User Preferences

Implementing user settings allows players to customize their gameplay
experience. Key settings may include graphics options, audio levels, control
mappings, and accessibility features.

## 3.2 Creating a User Settings Menu

1. **Designing the Settings UI**: Use UMG to create a user settings menu
   that allows players to adjust various options. Include sliders for volume,

dropdowns for graphics settings, and buttons for control mappings.

2. **Binding Settings to Variables**: In your settings menu, bind UI elements to C++ variables that represent user preferences.

```cpp
Copy code
UFUNCTION(BlueprintCallable, Category = "Settings")
void SetVolume(float NewVolume);
```

1. **Saving User Preferences**: Implement functionality to save user preferences using Unreal's Save Game system. Create a Save Game class to store these settings.

```cpp
Copy code
void UMyGameInstance::SaveUserSettings()
{
    USaveGameData* SaveGameInstance =
 Cast<USaveGameData>(UGameplayStatics:
:CreateSaveGameObject
(USaveGameData::StaticClass()));
    SaveGameInstance->Volume = CurrentVolume;
    SaveGameInstance->GraphicsQuality =
CurrentGraphicsQuality;

    UGameplayStatics::SaveGameToSlot
(SaveGameInstance, TEXT("UserSettings"), 0);
}
```

## 3.3 Loading User Preferences

1. **Loading Settings on Start**: When the game starts, load the saved user preferences and apply them to the game settings. This ensures that players' settings are retained across sessions.

```cpp
Copy code
void UMyGameInstance::LoadUserSettings()
{
    USaveGameData* LoadGameInstance =
 Cast<USaveGameData>(UGameplayStatics:
:LoadGameFromSlot
(TEXT("UserSettings"), 0));
    if (LoadGameInstance)
    {
        CurrentVolume =
 LoadGameInstance->Volume;
        CurrentGraphicsQuality =
 LoadGameInstance->GraphicsQuality;
    }
}
```

## Section 4: Preparing for Different Platforms

### 4.1 Platform-Specific Considerations

When preparing your game for release, consider the specific requirements and guidelines for each platform (PC, consoles, mobile).

1. **Performance Optimization**: Optimize your game for the target platform's hardware specifications. For example, mobile games may require lower resolutions and simplified graphics.
2. **Input Management**: Ensure that your game supports various input methods. For example, console games should support gamepad input, while PC games may require keyboard and mouse controls.

### 4.2 Packaging for Different Platforms

1. **Platform-Specific Packaging**: Use the *Package Project* option in Unreal Engine to create builds for each target platform. Ensure that you

configure settings specific to each platform.

2. **Testing on Target Platforms**: Thoroughly test your game on each target platform to identify and resolve any platform-specific issues.

## Section 5: Marketing Strategies for Your Game

### 5.1 Developing a Marketing Plan

A successful marketing strategy is essential for generating interest in your game. Develop a plan that outlines your target audience, marketing channels, and promotional activities.

1. **Identifying Your Target Audience**: Understand who your game appeals to and tailor your marketing messages accordingly. Consider demographics, interests, and gaming preferences.
2. **Choosing Marketing Channels**: Select the most effective channels for reaching your audience, including social media, gaming forums, and influencer partnerships.

### 5.2 Creating Promotional Material

1. **Trailers and Gameplay Videos**: Produce high-quality trailers that showcase your game's features and gameplay mechanics. These videos can be shared on platforms like YouTube and social media.
2. **Screenshots and Art Assets**: Capture engaging screenshots and create promotional art assets to use in marketing materials. Ensure these images highlight the game's unique aspects.

### 5.3 Engaging with the Community

1. **Building a Community**: Engage with players through social media, forums, and Discord. Create a community around your game to foster loyalty and gather feedback.
2. **Hosting Events**: Consider hosting events such as livestreams, Q&A

sessions, or beta tests to generate excitement and involve players in the development process.

## Section 6: Launching Your Game

### 6.1 Preparing for Launch Day

As launch day approaches, ensure that all aspects of your game are ready for public consumption.

1. **Final Checks**: Perform a final round of testing to catch any last-minute issues. Confirm that all marketing materials are in place and that your community is engaged and informed about the launch.
2. **Set Up Distribution Platforms**: Ensure that your game is set up for distribution on platforms such as Steam, Epic Games Store, or console stores. Familiarize yourself with their submission processes and requirements.

### 6.2 Post-Launch Support

1. **Monitoring Player Feedback**: After the game launches, actively monitor player feedback and reviews. Use this information to identify areas for improvement or bugs that need addressing.
2. **Implementing Updates**: Plan for post-launch updates to address bugs, balance gameplay, and add new content based on player feedback. Keep your community informed about upcoming updates and changes.

## Conclusion of Chapter 10

Congratulations on completing Chapter 10! You have gained a comprehensive understanding of how to prepare your game for release using Unreal Engine and C++. From finalizing gameplay features and optimizing performance to implementing user settings and marketing strategies, you now have the skills necessary to launch your game successfully.

In the next chapter, we will explore how to analyze player data and implement game analytics to improve player engagement and retention. Your journey through Unreal Engine and C++ is progressing well, and you are well on your way to mastering game development.

This chapter provides a thorough exploration of preparing your game for release in Unreal Engine using C++. It covers key aspects such as finalizing gameplay features, building configurations, implementing user settings, preparing for different platforms, and marketing strategies, equipping readers with the skills necessary to launch their games successfully.

/

# Chapter 11: Analyzing Player Data and Implementing Game Analytics

I n today's competitive gaming market, understanding player behavior and preferences is essential for success. Game analytics provides valuable insights into how players interact with your game, enabling developers to make data-driven decisions for improving gameplay, enhancing user experiences, and maximizing engagement. In this chapter, we will explore the importance of player data analysis, the implementation of game analytics systems in Unreal Engine, and best practices for interpreting and acting on data insights.

By the end of this chapter, you will have a comprehensive understanding of how to effectively collect and analyze player data, allowing you to refine your game and increase its appeal to your audience.

## Section 1: Understanding Game Analytics

### 1.1 What is Game Analytics?

Game analytics involves collecting, analyzing, and interpreting data generated by players during their gameplay sessions. This data can provide insights into player behavior, preferences, and challenges, informing decisions that enhance the overall gaming experience.

**Key Components of Game Analytics**:

- **Data Collection**: Gathering quantitative and qualitative data from gameplay sessions.
- **Data Analysis**: Analyzing the collected data to identify patterns, trends, and player behaviors.
- **Actionable Insights**: Using the analysis to inform game design decisions, improve features, and optimize user experiences.

### 1.2 Importance of Game Analytics

Understanding the importance of game analytics is crucial for making informed decisions that positively impact your game:

- **Improving Player Retention**: Analyzing player behavior can reveal why players leave and help implement strategies to keep them engaged.
- **Balancing Gameplay**: Data can highlight areas of difficulty or imbalance, enabling developers to adjust game mechanics for a better experience.
- **Enhancing Monetization**: Analytics can identify which features drive revenue, allowing for targeted improvements in monetization strategies.
- **Informed Updates**: Data-driven decisions can guide the development of new content and features based on player preferences.

## Section 2: Setting Up Analytics in Unreal Engine

### 2.1 Choosing an Analytics Solution

Before implementing analytics, it's essential to choose an appropriate solution that fits your game's needs. Some popular analytics platforms for Unreal Engine include:

- **Google Analytics**: A widely used web analytics tool that can be adapted for games.
- **GameAnalytics**: A dedicated analytics platform for games that provides event tracking and player metrics.
- **Unity Analytics**: Although originally for Unity, it can be used with Unreal via custom integrations.

## 2.2 Integrating Analytics SDKs

1. **Adding SDKs to Your Project**: Depending on the analytics solution chosen, follow the integration guidelines provided by the platform. This usually involves adding the SDK to your Unreal project through plugins or custom code.

- For example, to integrate GameAnalytics:
- Download the GameAnalytics SDK.
- Import the SDK into your Unreal project.
- Set up the necessary configurations in your project settings.

1. **Initializing Analytics in C++**: Initialize the analytics system in your game's main module or game instance to ensure it starts tracking when the game launches.

```cpp
Copy code
void UMyGameInstance::Init()
{
    Super::Init();
    GameAnalytics::Initialize();
}
```

## 2.3 Configuring Analytics Events

1. **Defining Key Events**: Determine which player actions you want to track. Common events include:

- Player progress (level completion, achievements)
- In-game purchases
- Gameplay sessions (start, end)
- User interactions (menu navigation, button clicks)

1. **Implementing Event Tracking**: Use the analytics SDK to send events based on player actions.

```cpp
Copy code
void AMyCharacter::TrackLevelComplete()
{
    GameAnalytics::AddEvent("LevelComplete", CurrentLevel);
}

void AMyCharacter::TrackPurchase
(const FString& ItemName)
{
    GameAnalytics::AddEvent
("ItemPurchased", ItemName);
}
```

## Section 3: Analyzing Player Data

### 3.1 Understanding the Data Collected

Once you've implemented analytics, you can start collecting data. Understand the types of data you'll receive and how they can be interpreted.

- **Player Engagement Metrics**: Track session lengths, frequency of play, and player retention rates.
- **Behavioral Patterns**: Analyze how players interact with game features, such as inventory usage or combat actions.
- **Monetization Data**: Monitor in-game purchases, revenue generated from ads, and user spending habits.

### 3.2 Using Analytics Dashboards

Most analytics platforms provide dashboards to visualize collected data. Familiarize yourself with these tools:

1. **Visualizing Metrics**: Use graphs and charts to analyze trends over time, such as player retention rates or session lengths.
2. **Segmenting Data**: Segment data by different player demographics (age, region) to identify which groups are most engaged or successful.
3. **3 Interpreting Data Insights**
4. **Identifying Trends**: Look for patterns in player behavior. For example, if players consistently drop off after a particular level, investigate that level's design and difficulty.
5. **Gathering Feedback**: Combine analytics data with qualitative feedback from players to gain a holistic view of their experiences.

## Section 4: Implementing Data-Driven Design Changes

### 4.1 Making Informed Design Decisions

Use the insights gathered from analytics to make data-driven decisions regarding your game design:

1. **Balancing Game Mechanics**: Adjust difficulty based on player progress and drop-off rates. If many players fail at a specific challenge, consider adjusting its difficulty or providing additional resources.
2. **Enhancing Features**: If a particular feature (e.g., crafting system) shows high engagement, consider expanding it with more options or rewards.

### 4.2 Conducting A/B Testing

A/B testing is a method of comparing two versions of a game feature to determine which one performs better.

1. **Setting Up A/B Tests**: Create two variations of a feature (e.g., two different user interface designs) and track player interactions with both.
2. **Analyzing Results**: Use analytics data to determine which version leads to better player engagement, retention, or satisfaction.

## Section 5: Addressing Player Feedback

### 5.1 Gathering Player Feedback

While analytics provides quantitative data, qualitative feedback from players is equally important. Gather feedback through:

- **Surveys**: Implement in-game surveys or use external platforms to collect player opinions.
- **Social Media and Forums**: Monitor discussions about your game on platforms like Reddit, Discord, and Twitter.

### 5.2 Responding to Feedback

1. **Identifying Common Themes**: Look for recurring themes in player feedback. If multiple players mention a specific issue, prioritize addressing it.
2. **Implementing Changes**: Communicate with your community about changes being made based on their feedback. This engagement builds trust and encourages further feedback.

## Section 6: Ethical Considerations in Analytics

### 6.1 Understanding Player Privacy

When collecting player data, it's essential to consider privacy and ethical implications:

1. **Data Collection Transparency**: Be transparent with players about what data you collect and how it will be used. Provide clear privacy policies.
2. **Consent**: Obtain consent from players before collecting their data, particularly in regions where data protection laws (like GDPR) apply.

### 6.2 Analyzing Data Responsibly

1. **Avoiding Overreach**: Collect only the data necessary for your analytics. Avoid invasive tracking methods that could damage player trust.
2. **Protecting Player Data**: Implement robust security measures to protect player data from breaches or misuse.

## Conclusion of Chapter 11

Congratulations on completing Chapter 11! You have gained a comprehensive understanding of how to analyze player data and implement game analytics in Unreal Engine using C++. From setting up analytics systems and tracking player interactions to interpreting data insights and making informed design changes, you are now equipped with the tools necessary to enhance your game based on player behavior and preferences.

In the next chapter, we will explore advanced topics such as modding support, user-generated content, and how to foster a community around your game. Your journey through Unreal Engine and C++ is progressing well, and you are well on your way to mastering game development.

This chapter provides a thorough exploration of analyzing player data and implementing game analytics in Unreal Engine using C++. It covers the fundamentals of analytics, setting up systems, interpreting data, and making informed design decisions, equipping readers with the skills necessary to improve gameplay experiences based on player insights.

# Chapter 12: Supporting Modding and User-Generated Content

I
n the gaming industry, modding and user-generated content (UGC) have become increasingly important. They not only extend the lifespan of a game but also foster a dedicated community around it. By allowing players to create and share their own content, developers can enhance player engagement, create new experiences, and build a loyal fan base. In this chapter, we will explore how to support modding and user-generated content in your Unreal Engine projects, including best practices, tools, and implementation strategies.

By the end of this chapter, you will have a thorough understanding of how to design your game to accommodate modding and UGC, ensuring a vibrant community and extended gameplay experience.

## Section 1: Understanding Modding and User-Generated Content

### 1.1 What is Modding?

Modding refers to the practice of modifying a game to create new content or alter existing content. This can include changes to gameplay mechanics, new characters, levels, or even entirely new games based on the original. Modding can be done by players or developers and is often encouraged by the game creators.

### 1.2 Importance of Modding and UGC

1. **Increased Longevity**: Modding extends the life of a game by introducing new content and keeping the community engaged.
2. **Player Engagement**: Providing tools for modding allows players to express their creativity, fostering a sense of ownership and investment in the game.
3. **Community Building**: Games that support modding often have vibrant communities that share content, collaborate on projects, and provide feedback to developers.

## Section 2: Designing Your Game for Modding

### 2.1 Planning for Modding Support

When developing your game, consider how modding will fit into your design from the beginning. This includes identifying which aspects of your game can be modified or expanded by users.

1. **Identify Core Components**: Determine which components are essential for modding, such as assets (models, textures), gameplay mechanics, and level design.
2. **Define Modding Scope**: Decide how much of the game you want to allow players to modify. This could range from simple skin changes to complete overhauls of game mechanics.

### 2.2 Modular Game Design

Creating a modular game design is crucial for supporting modding.

1. **Asset Management**: Organize your assets in a way that makes them easy for modders to access and modify. Use a clear folder structure in the Content Browser.
2. **Scripting and Extensibility**: Use Unreal Engine's Blueprint system to allow modders to script gameplay changes. This can enable non-

programmers to create new game features.

## Section 3: Tools for Modding Support

### 3.1 Unreal Engine's Modding Tools
Unreal Engine provides several built-in tools to facilitate modding:

1. **Content Browser**: Use the Content Browser to manage and organize assets, making it easier for modders to find and modify game elements.
2. **Blueprints**: Allow modders to create new gameplay mechanics without requiring C++ knowledge. This makes it accessible for a wider audience.
3. **Level Editor**: Enable modders to design new levels using the same powerful tools available to developers.

### 3.2 Providing an SDK
Consider providing a Software Development Kit (SDK) for your game. An SDK includes documentation, example projects, and the necessary tools for modders to create new content.

1. **Documentation**: Provide comprehensive documentation detailing how to use your game's modding features, including examples of common tasks.
2. **Example Projects**: Include example projects that demonstrate how to create mods using your tools and assets.

## Section 4: Creating a Modding Community

### 4.1 Building a Platform for Mod Sharing
To encourage modding, create a platform where users can share their creations.

1. **Official Website or Forum**: Set up an official website or forum where modders can share their work, ask questions, and collaborate with

others.

2. **Modding Contests**: Host contests to encourage creativity and recognize outstanding mods. This can foster a sense of community and competition among players.

### 4.2 Engaging with Your Community

1. **Feedback Loop**: Actively engage with the modding community, gathering feedback on modding tools and addressing issues they encounter.
2. **Showcase Player Creations**: Highlight popular mods or content created by players to encourage others to participate and create.

## Section 5: Implementing Modding Support in Your Game

### 5.1 Creating a Modding Framework

1. **Setting Up Mod Folders**: Create a folder structure for mods within your game directory. This allows players to easily install and manage their mods without modifying core game files.
2. **Loading Mods at Runtime**: Implement functionality to load mods dynamically when the game starts. This can be done by scanning the mod folders and integrating the assets and scripts into the game.

```cpp
Copy code
void AMyGameMode::LoadMods()
{
    // Code to scan for mods and load them into the game
}
```

### 5.2 Allowing Custom Assets

1. **Importing Custom Models and Textures**: Provide modders with

guidelines on how to import their custom models and textures into the game. Ensure that the game can recognize and load these assets at runtime.

2. **Handling Asset Conflicts**: Implement a system to manage asset conflicts. For example, if two mods use the same asset name, allow the player to choose which one to use or provide a resolution system.

## Section 6: Testing and Supporting Mods

### 6.1 Quality Assurance for Mods

1. **Testing Mods**: Encourage modders to test their content thoroughly before releasing it. Provide them with tools and guidelines for testing mod compatibility with the base game.
2. **Bug Reporting System**: Set up a bug reporting system for mods, allowing players to report issues that arise from using specific mods.

### 6.2 Ongoing Support for Modding

1. **Regular Updates**: Keep your modding tools and documentation up to date with regular game updates. Ensure that modders know how to adapt their content to any changes made to the base game.
2. **Community Moderation**: If your game allows players to share mods, implement a moderation system to ensure that content is appropriate and functions as intended.

## Section 7: Marketing Your Modding Capabilities

### 7.1 Promoting Mod Support

1. **Showcasing Mods**: Use your marketing channels to showcase popular mods or user-generated content. Highlighting these creations can attract new players interested in the potential for customization.

2. **Creating Tutorials**: Develop tutorials and guides on how to mod your game effectively. This can help demystify the process for players who may be hesitant to try.

### 7.2 Leveraging Influencers and Content Creators

1. **Collaborate with Influencers**: Reach out to gaming influencers who specialize in modding or user-generated content. Having them showcase your game's modding capabilities can generate interest and attract a dedicated audience.
2. **Encourage Streamers**: Encourage streamers to explore mods on their channels. This exposure can lead to increased engagement and new players discovering the game.

## *Conclusion of Chapter 12*

Congratulations on completing Chapter 12! You have learned how to support modding and user-generated content in your Unreal Engine projects using C++. From designing your game for modding and providing tools for creators to building a community and marketing your modding capabilities, you now possess the knowledge necessary to foster a vibrant and engaged player base.

In the next chapter, we will explore how to analyze player data and implement game analytics to improve player engagement and retention. Your journey through Unreal Engine and C++ is progressing well, and you are well on your way to mastering game development.

This chapter provides a thorough exploration of supporting modding and user-generated content in Unreal Engine using C++. It covers the design considerations, implementation strategies, community building, and marketing efforts necessary to create a successful modding environment, equipping readers with the skills needed to enhance their game's longevity and engagement through user-generated content.

# Chapter 13: Analyzing Player Data and Implementing Game Analytics

I n the modern gaming industry, understanding player behavior and preferences is essential for success. Game analytics provides valuable insights into how players interact with your game, enabling developers to make data-driven decisions for improving gameplay, enhancing user experiences, and maximizing engagement. In this chapter, we will explore the importance of player data analysis, the implementation of game analytics systems in Unreal Engine, and best practices for interpreting and acting on data insights.

By the end of this chapter, you will have a comprehensive understanding of how to effectively collect and analyze player data, allowing you to refine your game and increase its appeal to your audience.

## Section 1: Understanding Game Analytics

### 1.1 What is Game Analytics?

Game analytics involves collecting, analyzing, and interpreting data generated by players during their gameplay sessions. This data can provide insights into player behavior, preferences, and challenges, informing decisions that enhance the overall gaming experience.

**Key Components of Game Analytics**:

- **Data Collection**: Gathering quantitative and qualitative data from gameplay sessions.
- **Data Analysis**: Analyzing the collected data to identify patterns, trends, and player behaviors.
- **Actionable Insights**: Using the analysis to inform game design decisions, improve features, and optimize user experiences.

### 1.2 Importance of Game Analytics

Understanding the importance of game analytics is crucial for making informed decisions that positively impact your game:

- **Improving Player Retention**: Analyzing player behavior can reveal why players leave and help implement strategies to keep them engaged.
- **Balancing Gameplay**: Data can highlight areas of difficulty or imbalance, enabling developers to adjust game mechanics for a better experience.
- **Enhancing Monetization**: Analytics can identify which features drive revenue, allowing for targeted improvements in monetization strategies.
- **Informed Updates**: Data-driven decisions can guide the development of new content and features based on player preferences.

## Section 2: Setting Up Analytics in Unreal Engine

### 2.1 Choosing an Analytics Solution

Before implementing analytics, it's essential to choose an appropriate solution that fits your game's needs. Some popular analytics platforms for Unreal Engine include:

- **Google Analytics**: A widely used web analytics tool that can be adapted for games.
- **GameAnalytics**: A dedicated analytics platform for games that provides event tracking and player metrics.
- **PlayFab**: A complete backend platform that includes analytics and player data management.

## 2.2 Integrating Analytics SDKs

1. **Adding SDKs to Your Project**: Depending on the analytics solution chosen, follow the integration guidelines provided by the platform. This usually involves adding the SDK to your Unreal project through plugins or custom code.

- For example, to integrate GameAnalytics:
- Download the GameAnalytics SDK.
- Import the SDK into your Unreal project.
- Set up the necessary configurations in your project settings.

1. **Initializing Analytics in C++**: Initialize the analytics system in your game's main module or game instance to ensure it starts tracking when the game launches.

```cpp
Copy code
void UMyGameInstance::Init()
{
    Super::Init();
    GameAnalytics::Initialize();
}
```

## 2.3 Configuring Analytics Events

1. **Defining Key Events**: Determine which player actions you want to track. Common events include:

- Player progress (level completion, achievements)
- In-game purchases
- Gameplay sessions (start, end)
- User interactions (menu navigation, button clicks)

1. **Implementing Event Tracking**: Use the analytics SDK to send events based on player actions.

```cpp
Copy code
void AMyCharacter::TrackLevelComplete()
{
    GameAnalytics::AddEvent("LevelComplete", CurrentLevel);
}

void AMyCharacter::TrackPurchase(const FString& ItemName)
{
    GameAnalytics::AddEvent("ItemPurchased", ItemName);
}
```

## Section 3: Analyzing Player Data

### 3.1 Understanding the Data Collected

Once you've implemented analytics, you can start collecting data. Understand the types of data you'll receive and how they can be interpreted.

- **Player Engagement Metrics**: Track session lengths, frequency of play, and player retention rates.
- **Behavioral Patterns**: Analyze how players interact with game features, such as inventory usage or combat actions.
- **Monetization Data**: Monitor in-game purchases, revenue generated from ads, and user spending habits.

### 3.2 Using Analytics Dashboards

Most analytics platforms provide dashboards to visualize collected data. Familiarize yourself with these tools:

1. **Visualizing Metrics**: Use graphs and charts to analyze trends over time,

such as player retention rates or session lengths.

2. **Segmenting Data**: Segment data by different player demographics (age, region) to identify which groups are most engaged or successful.
3. **3 Interpreting Data Insights**
4. **Identifying Trends**: Look for patterns in player behavior. For example, if players consistently drop off after a particular level, investigate that level's design and difficulty.
5. **Gathering Feedback**: Combine analytics data with qualitative feedback from players to gain a holistic view of their experiences.

## Section 4: Implementing Data-Driven Design Changes

### 4.1 Making Informed Design Decisions

Use the insights gathered from analytics to make data-driven decisions regarding your game design:

1. **Balancing Game Mechanics**: Adjust difficulty based on player progress and drop-off rates. If many players fail at a specific challenge, consider adjusting its difficulty or providing additional resources.
2. **Enhancing Features**: If a particular feature (e.g., crafting system) shows high engagement, consider expanding it with more options or rewards.

### 4.2 Conducting A/B Testing

A/B testing is a method of comparing two versions of a game feature to determine which one performs better.

1. **Setting Up A/B Tests**: Create two variations of a feature (e.g., two different user interface designs) and track player interactions with both.
2. **Analyzing Results**: Use analytics data to determine which version leads to better player engagement, retention, or satisfaction.

## Section 5: Addressing Player Feedback

### 5.1 Gathering Player Feedback

While analytics provides quantitative data, qualitative feedback from players is equally important. Gather feedback through:

- **Surveys**: Implement in-game surveys or use external platforms to collect player opinions.
- **Social Media and Forums**: Monitor discussions about your game on platforms like Reddit, Discord, and Twitter.

### 5.2 Responding to Feedback

1. **Identifying Common Themes**: Look for recurring themes in player feedback. If multiple players mention a specific issue, prioritize addressing it.
2. **Implementing Changes**: Communicate with your community about changes being made based on their feedback. This engagement builds trust and encourages further feedback.

## Section 6: Ethical Considerations in Analytics

### 6.1 Understanding Player Privacy

When collecting player data, it's essential to consider privacy and ethical implications:

1. **Data Collection Transparency**: Be transparent with players about what data you collect and how it will be used. Provide clear privacy policies.
2. **Consent**: Obtain consent from players before collecting their data, particularly in regions where data protection laws (like GDPR) apply.

### 6.2 Analyzing Data Responsibly

1. **Avoiding Overreach**: Collect only the data necessary for your analytics. Avoid invasive tracking methods that could damage player trust.
2. **Protecting Player Data**: Implement robust security measures to protect player data from breaches or misuse.

## *Conclusion of Chapter 13*

Congratulations on completing Chapter 13! You have gained a comprehensive understanding of how to analyze player data and implement game analytics in Unreal Engine using C++. From setting up analytics systems and tracking player interactions to interpreting data insights and making informed design changes, you are now equipped with the tools necessary to enhance gameplay experiences based on player insights.

In the next chapter, we will explore advanced topics such as modding support, user-generated content, and how to foster a community around your game. Your journey through Unreal Engine and C++ is progressing well, and you are well on your way to mastering game development.

This chapter provides a thorough exploration of analyzing player data and implementing game analytics in Unreal Engine using C++. It covers the fundamentals of analytics, setting up systems, interpreting data, and making informed design decisions, equipping readers with the skills necessary to improve gameplay experiences based on player insights.

# Chapter 14: Enhancing Your Game with User-Generated Content and Modding Support

Ser-generated content (UGC) and modding have become critical elements in modern game design, fostering vibrant communities and extending the lifespan of games. By empowering players to create and share their content, developers can significantly enhance engagement and enjoyment. This chapter will guide you through the implementation of UGC and modding support in your Unreal Engine project, including best practices, tools, and strategies to foster a thriving modding community.

*Section 1: Understanding User-Generated Content*

### 1.1 What is User-Generated Content?

User-generated content refers to any content created by players rather than the developers themselves. This can include new levels, characters, mods, art, scripts, and other modifications that alter or expand the game experience.

### 1.2 Importance of UGC and Modding

1. **Extended Game Longevity**: UGC can keep players engaged long after the initial release by introducing fresh experiences and content.

2. **Community Engagement**: Allowing players to create their content fosters a sense of community, leading to increased player loyalty and engagement.

3. **Increased Replayability**: Modding can provide endless replayability, as players can create their scenarios and challenges.

## Section 2: Designing Your Game for Modding Support

### 2.1 Planning for Modding Support

When developing your game, consider how you will facilitate modding. This includes deciding which elements of your game should be modifiable and how players can create and implement their mods.

1. **Identifying Modifiable Elements**: Determine which aspects of your game will allow modifications. Common elements include:

- Levels and environments
- Game mechanics and rules
- Characters and skins
- Audio and visual assets

1. **Creating a Mod-Friendly Architecture**: Your game's architecture should support easy modifications. This includes:

- Clear separation between core game files and modifiable assets.
- Flexible systems that allow modders to extend or override existing functionality.

### 2.2 Modular Game Design

A modular design approach allows you to create components that can be easily replaced or extended by mods.

1. **Creating Asset Bundles**: Organize assets into bundles that can be

independently loaded or replaced. For example, create bundles for textures, audio, and scripts.

2. **Scripting Interfaces**: Expose certain gameplay elements through scripting interfaces, enabling modders to create new gameplay mechanics without modifying the core game code.

## Section 3: Implementing Modding Tools and SDKs

### 3.1 Providing Development Tools

To empower your community, provide tools and documentation that enable players to create their mods easily.

1. **Custom Editor**: Consider developing a simplified editor for modding that allows users to create and modify levels, scripts, and assets without needing deep programming knowledge.
2. **Sample Content**: Include sample content and templates in your SDK to help modders get started quickly.
3. **2 SDK Documentation**
4. **Comprehensive Documentation**: Create detailed documentation that explains how to use the tools and systems provided. This should cover:

- Asset creation guidelines
- Scripting tutorials
- Packaging and distributing mods

1. **Tutorials and Examples**: Provide video tutorials and example projects that showcase how to create various types of mods. This will help users understand the process and inspire creativity.

## Section 4: Building a Modding Community

### 4.1 Establishing Platforms for Sharing

Create a platform where users can share their mods, collaborate, and discuss ideas. This could be an official website, forum, or a dedicated Discord server.

1. **Mod Repository**: Implement a mod repository where players can upload, download, and review mods. Include tagging systems and categories to organize content effectively.
2. **Discussion Forums**: Establish forums where players can ask questions, share tips, and collaborate on modding projects.

### 4.2 Engaging with Your Community

1. **Encourage Feedback**: Regularly engage with the community to gather feedback on your modding tools and systems. Be open to suggestions for improvement.
2. **Highlighting Player Creations**: Showcase outstanding mods created by players on your official channels. This recognition can motivate others to contribute.

### 4.3 Hosting Modding Contests

1. **Organizing Contests**: Host modding contests to encourage creativity and competition among your players. Offer prizes or recognition for the best mods.
2. **Promoting Participation**: Use your community platforms to promote these contests and share the results, inspiring further participation in modding activities.

## Section 5: Implementing UGC Features in Your Game

### 5.1 Allowing Custom Assets

1. **Importing Custom Models and Textures**: Provide clear guidelines on how players can create and import their custom models and textures into the game.
2. **Asset Management Systems**: Implement systems that allow players to manage their assets effectively. This could include asset directories or libraries that track imported content.

### 5.2 Loading Mods at Runtime

1. **Dynamic Mod Loading**: Implement functionality to load mods dynamically when the game starts. This could involve scanning designated mod folders and integrating assets and scripts into the game.

```cpp
Copy code
void AMyGameMode::LoadMods()
{
    // Code to scan for mods and load them into the game
}
```

1. **Handling Asset Conflicts**: Create a system for managing asset conflicts, allowing players to choose which versions of assets to load if there are duplicates.

## Section 6: Testing and Supporting Mods

### 6.1 Quality Assurance for Mods

1. **Testing Community Mods**: Consider implementing a QA process for popular mods to ensure they work well with the base game. This can help maintain the quality of content available to players.
2. **Feedback Mechanism**: Provide a way for players to report bugs or issues with specific mods. This can help both modders and players resolve conflicts.

### 6.2 Ongoing Support for Modding

1. **Regular Updates**: Keep your modding tools and documentation updated with each game update. Ensure that modders know how to adapt their content to any changes made to the base game.
2. **Community Moderation**: If your game allows players to share mods, implement a moderation system to ensure that content is appropriate and functions as intended.

## Section 7: Marketing Your Modding Capabilities

### 7.1 Promoting Mod Support

1. **Showcasing Mods**: Use your marketing channels to showcase popular mods or user-generated content. Highlighting these creations can attract new players interested in the potential for customization.
2. **Creating Tutorials**: Develop tutorials and guides on how to mod your game effectively. This can help demystify the process for players who may be hesitant to try.

### 7.2 Leveraging Influencers and Content Creators

1. **Collaborate with Influencers**: Reach out to gaming influencers who specialize in modding or user-generated content. Having them showcase your game's modding capabilities can generate interest and attract a dedicated audience.
2. **Encourage Streamers**: Encourage streamers to explore mods on their channels. This exposure can lead to increased engagement and new players discovering the game.

## Section 8: Measuring the Impact of UGC

### 8.1 Analyzing UGC Data

1. **Tracking UGC Usage**: Implement analytics to track the usage of user-generated content. Measure how often mods are downloaded and played, and gather feedback on their impact on gameplay.
2. **Identifying Popular Content**: Use analytics to identify which mods are most popular and which types of content engage players the most.

### 8.2 Iterating on Modding Support

1. **Using Data to Improve Tools**: Analyze data to inform improvements to your modding tools and systems. If certain aspects are underutilized, consider how to make them more accessible or appealing to players.
2. **Community Feedback**: Regularly solicit feedback from the community about their modding experiences. Use this feedback to make targeted improvements to the modding process.

## Conclusion of Chapter 14

Congratulations on completing Chapter 14! You have learned how to enhance your game with user-generated content and modding support in Unreal Engine using C++. From designing your game for modding and providing tools for creators to building a community and marketing your modding capabilities, you now possess the knowledge necessary to foster a vibrant and engaged player base.

In the next chapter, we will explore the process of monetizing your game, including strategies for in-game purchases, DLCs, and other revenue models. Your journey through Unreal Engine and C++ is progressing well, and you are well on your way to mastering game development.

This chapter provides a thorough exploration of enhancing your game with user-generated content and modding support in Unreal Engine using C++. It covers the design considerations, implementation strategies, community building, and marketing efforts necessary to create a successful modding environment, equipping readers with the skills needed to enhance their game's longevity and engagement through user-generated content.

# Chapter 15: Monetizing Your Game: Strategies and Best Practices

As a game developer, monetization is a critical aspect of your project's success. While the primary goal is often to create an engaging and enjoyable experience for players, ensuring that your game is financially viable is essential for sustainability and growth. In this chapter, we will explore various monetization strategies for your game, including in-game purchases, downloadable content (DLC), subscription models, and advertising. We will also discuss best practices for implementing these strategies effectively and ethically.

By the end of this chapter, you will have a comprehensive understanding of how to monetize your game while maintaining player satisfaction and trust.

*Section 1: Understanding Monetization Models*

### 1.1 Overview of Monetization Models

There are several monetization models that developers can choose from, each with its advantages and disadvantages. Understanding these models is crucial for selecting the right approach for your game.

1. **Premium Pricing**: Players pay a one-time fee to purchase the game. This model is straightforward and can generate immediate revenue.

2. **Freemium Model**: The game is free to play, but players can make in-game purchases to enhance their experience (e.g., cosmetic items, power-ups).
3. **Subscription Model**: Players pay a recurring fee (monthly or annually) to access the game or specific content.
4. **In-Game Advertising**: Display ads within the game, generating revenue based on impressions or clicks.
5. **Downloadable Content (DLC)**: Players can purchase additional content that expands or enhances the base game.

### 1.2 Choosing the Right Monetization Strategy

The choice of monetization strategy depends on various factors, including your game type, target audience, and market trends. Consider the following when selecting a model:

- **Player Expectations**: Understand what your target audience expects in terms of pricing and monetization. For example, players of mobile games often expect freemium models, while console gamers may prefer premium pricing.
- **Game Genre**: Different genres may lend themselves better to specific monetization strategies. For instance, casual games often thrive on freemium models, while narrative-driven games might succeed with premium pricing.
- **Market Trends**: Stay informed about current trends in game monetization. Analyze successful games in your genre to understand their monetization approaches.

## Section 2: Implementing In-Game Purchases

### 2.1 Types of In-Game Purchases

In-game purchases can take various forms, allowing players to buy virtual goods, cosmetics, or enhancements that improve their gameplay experience.

1. **Cosmetic Items**: These items alter the appearance of characters or environments without affecting gameplay (e.g., skins, outfits).
2. **Power-Ups**: Consumable items that provide temporary boosts or advantages in gameplay (e.g., extra lives, speed boosts).
3. **Loot Boxes**: Players purchase boxes containing randomized items, offering both excitement and potential rewards.

## 2.2 Setting Up In-Game Purchases in Unreal Engine

1. **Integrating Payment Systems**: Choose a payment processing solution that suits your game. For mobile games, consider using Google Play or Apple's App Store for in-app purchases.
2. **Implementing Storefronts**: Create an in-game storefront where players can browse and purchase items. Use Unreal Engine's UMG (Unreal Motion Graphics) to design the UI for the storefront.

```cpp
Copy code
UFUNCTION(BlueprintCallable, Category = "Store")
void PurchaseItem(FString ItemID)
{
    // Logic to handle item purchase
}
```

1. **Tracking Purchases**: Implement functionality to track player purchases and update their inventories accordingly.

## 2.3 Best Practices for In-Game Purchases

1. **Transparency**: Clearly communicate the benefits and costs associated with in-game purchases. Avoid misleading players about the value of items.

2. **Avoiding Pay-to-Win Mechanics**: Ensure that in-game purchases do not create an unfair advantage for paying players. Focus on cosmetic items or convenience features instead.

3. **Regular Content Updates**: Keep the in-game store fresh by regularly adding new items and features, encouraging players to return and make purchases.

## Section 3: Downloadable Content (DLC)

### 3.1 What is DLC?

Downloadable content (DLC) refers to additional content that players can purchase to enhance or expand the base game. This can include new levels, characters, story content, or game modes.

### 3.2 Types of DLC

1. **Expansion Packs**: Large content additions that significantly alter or expand the game. Often includes new storylines, characters, and gameplay mechanics.

2. **Mini DLC**: Smaller content packs that add new features or items without dramatically changing the game.

3. **Season Passes**: Players pay a fee upfront for access to multiple DLC releases over a specific period.

### 3.3 Implementing DLC in Unreal Engine

1. **Creating DLC Packages**: Use Unreal Engine's packaging tools to create DLC packages. Ensure that they can be installed and recognized by the base game.

2. **Integrating with the Store**: Implement storefront functionality to allow players to purchase and download DLC directly from the game.

```cpp
Copy code
UFUNCTION(BlueprintCallable, Category = "DLC")
void PurchaseDLC(FString DLCID)
{
    // Logic to handle DLC purchase
}
```

1. **Tracking DLC Ownership**: Use Unreal's online subsystem to track which players own specific DLC packages, enabling access to additional content.

### 3.4 Best Practices for DLC

1. **Value for Money**: Ensure that the content provided in DLC offers good value for the price. Players should feel that they are receiving worthwhile additions.
2. **Communicating Content**: Clearly communicate what each DLC contains and how it enhances the gameplay experience. Use trailers, screenshots, and descriptions effectively.
3. **Timing of Releases**: Strategically time DLC releases to maintain player engagement. Consider releasing content that coincides with significant game updates or events.

## Section 4: Subscription Models

### 4.1 Understanding Subscription Models

Subscription models involve players paying a recurring fee to access a game or specific content. This model has gained popularity, especially in the realm of online games and services.

1. **Full Access Subscriptions**: Players pay a fee to access the entire game or service for a set period.

DEVELOP HIGH QUALITY VIDEO GAMES WITH C++ AND UNREAL

2. **Content-Only Subscriptions**: Players subscribe to access specific features or additional content while the base game remains free or paid separately.

## 4.2 Implementing Subscription Services in Unreal Engine

1. **Subscription Management**: Use third-party services (like PlayFab or Microsoft Azure) to manage subscriptions and payment processing.
2. **Integrating with Gameplay**: Ensure that subscription benefits are clearly defined within the game. This could include exclusive content, access to events, or premium features.

## 4.3 Best Practices for Subscription Models

1. **Trial Periods**: Consider offering trial periods for new players to experience the benefits of the subscription before committing.
2. **Transparent Pricing**: Clearly communicate the pricing structure and what players receive with their subscription.
3. **Regular Updates**: Keep subscribers engaged by regularly providing new content or features, encouraging them to maintain their subscriptions.

## Section 5: In-Game Advertising

### 5.1 Understanding In-Game Advertising

In-game advertising involves displaying ads within your game, generating revenue based on impressions or clicks. This model can be particularly effective in free-to-play games.

### 5.2 Types of In-Game Advertising

1. **Banner Ads**: Static or dynamic advertisements displayed in specific areas of the game interface.
2. **Interstitial Ads**: Full-screen ads that appear at natural transition points in gameplay, such as level changes or menu navigation.

3. **Rewarded Ads:** Players can choose to watch ads in exchange for in-game rewards, such as currency or items.

## 5.3 Implementing In-Game Advertising in Unreal Engine

1. **Ad Networks**: Integrate with ad networks (like AdMob, Unity Ads, or others) to manage and display advertisements in your game.
2. **Configuring Ad Placement**: Determine where and when ads will be displayed, ensuring they do not disrupt the gameplay experience.

```cpp
Copy code
void AMyGameMode::ShowInterstitialAd()
{
    // Code to show an interstitial ad
}
```

1. **Tracking Ad Performance**: Use analytics to track ad performance, including impressions, clicks, and player engagement.

## 5.4 Best Practices for In-Game Advertising

1. **Player Experience**: Ensure that ads do not detract from the overall player experience. Avoid excessive or intrusive advertising that may frustrate players.
2. **Testing Different Formats**: Experiment with different ad formats to find the most effective and least intrusive options for your game.
3. **Rewarding Players**: Consider implementing rewarded ads as an option for players. This provides an incentive for players to engage with ads without forcing them to do so.

## Section 6: Ethical Considerations in Monetization

### 6.1 Transparency and Trust

1. **Clear Communication**: Be transparent about monetization methods and how they affect gameplay. Players should understand what they are paying for and how it impacts their experience.
2. **Avoiding Misleading Practices**: Steer clear of misleading marketing practices that could lead players to feel deceived or frustrated.

### 6.2 Balancing Monetization and Gameplay

1. **Player-Centric Design**: Prioritize player experience in your monetization strategies. Ensure that monetization does not compromise the core gameplay experience.
2. **Ethical Pricing**: Set fair prices for in-game purchases and DLC. Avoid exploiting players through aggressive monetization tactics.

### 6.3 Adherence to Regulations

1. **Compliance with Laws**: Ensure compliance with laws and regulations regarding monetization, particularly in regions with strict consumer protection laws.
2. **Data Privacy**: Protect player data and comply with regulations such as GDPR when implementing monetization features that involve data collection.

## Section 7: Analyzing the Impact of Monetization Strategies

### 7.1 Tracking Revenue Metrics

1. **Analyzing Sales Data**: Regularly analyze sales data from in-game purchases, DLC, and subscriptions to understand revenue streams and

player spending habits.

2. **Using Analytics**: Use analytics tools to track player engagement with monetization features. Monitor how different strategies impact player retention and satisfaction.

### 7.2 Adapting to Player Behavior

1. **Player Feedback**: Gather feedback from players regarding monetization features. Use this information to make informed decisions about adjustments or improvements.
2. **Testing New Strategies**: Continuously test new monetization strategies and evaluate their effectiveness through analytics and player feedback.

## Conclusion of Chapter 15

Congratulations on completing Chapter 15! You have gained a comprehensive understanding of various monetization strategies for your game, including in-game purchases, downloadable content, subscription models, and advertising. You also learned about best practices for implementing these strategies effectively while maintaining player trust and satisfaction.

In the next chapter, we will explore how to analyze player data and implement game analytics to improve player engagement and retention. Your journey through Unreal Engine and C++ is progressing well, and you are well on your way to mastering game development.

This chapter provides a thorough exploration of monetization strategies and best practices in Unreal Engine using C++. It covers different monetization models, including in-game purchases, DLC, subscription services, and advertising, equipping readers with the knowledge to effectively monetize their games while maintaining player satisfaction.

# Conclusion

As we wrap up this journey through the intricate world of game development with Unreal Engine and C++, we reflect on the skills, knowledge, and insights you've gained throughout the chapters. Creating a high-quality video game is a multifaceted endeavor that combines technical prowess, creative vision, and an understanding of player engagement. The foundation laid in this book equips you to embark on your own game development projects, whether you are a beginner or an experienced developer seeking to enhance your skills.

*Key Takeaways*

1. **Foundational Knowledge**: We began by exploring the fundamentals of Unreal Engine and C++. Understanding the engine's architecture and the basics of C++ programming forms the cornerstone of your game development journey. Mastering these foundational elements empowers you to build complex systems and mechanics, setting the stage for more advanced topics.

2. **Gameplay Mechanics and Systems**: As we delved into implementing gameplay mechanics, you learned to create engaging experiences that resonate with players. From developing character controls to crafting intricate gameplay systems, you now possess the tools to bring your game ideas to life. Remember, the key to a captivating gameplay experience

lies in understanding your audience and continually iterating based on feedback.

3. **Optimizing Performance**: In a world where players expect seamless experiences, optimizing your game's performance is crucial. The techniques discussed in this book—such as LOD, culling, and efficient memory management—are essential for creating a polished product. Performance profiling and testing will ensure that your game runs smoothly across various platforms and devices.

4. **Monetization Strategies**: We explored various monetization models and best practices to ensure your game is financially viable. Whether you choose in-game purchases, downloadable content, or a subscription model, it's essential to balance profitability with player satisfaction. Ethical monetization fosters trust and loyalty, leading to a more engaged player community.

5. **User-Generated Content and Modding Support**: Supporting modding and user-generated content can significantly enhance your game's longevity and community engagement. By providing tools and resources for players to create their content, you cultivate a vibrant ecosystem that keeps players invested in your game long after its initial release.

6. **Analytics and Player Data**: Understanding player behavior through analytics is paramount for refining your game. The ability to analyze data and respond to player needs allows you to make informed decisions that improve gameplay experiences and retention rates. Data-driven development can guide your design choices and ensure your game evolves with player expectations.

## Looking Forward

As you move forward in your game development journey, remember that the landscape is ever-changing. The gaming industry continues to evolve with advancements in technology, shifts in player preferences, and emerging platforms. Stay curious, be adaptable, and embrace continuous learning.

Engage with the community of developers, share your projects, seek feedback, and collaborate on new ideas. Attend game development conferences, participate in online forums, and explore the vast array of resources available. The journey of game development is not just about creating games but about building connections and sharing experiences.

## Final Thoughts

Creating a high-quality video game is both an art and a science. It requires creativity, dedication, and a willingness to learn and adapt. With the knowledge and skills gained from this book, you are well-prepared to tackle the challenges of game development head-on.

Whether you aim to create a solo indie project or join a larger studio, remember that each line of code you write, every design decision you make, and all the feedback you receive contribute to the greater tapestry of interactive entertainment.

Thank you for embarking on this journey with us. We hope this book has inspired you to create, innovate, and share your unique vision with the world. Your adventure in game development begins now, and we can't wait to see the incredible experiences you will bring to life.

www.ingramcontent.com/pod-product-compliance
Lightning Source LLC
LaVergne TN
LVHW051342050326
832903LV00031B/3688